Excellence In MINISTRY

Excellence In MINISTRY

Twelve Flagship Congregations Tell Their Story

C.S.S. Publishing Co., Inc.

Lima, Ohio

EXCELLENCE IN MINISTRY

Library of Congress Cataloging-in-Publication Data

Excellence in ministry.

1. Theology, Practical — Case studies. 2. Protestant churches — United States — Case studies. I. Title.
BV4.E93 1987 253'.0973 86-28360
ISBN 0-89536-866-8

7825 / ISBN 0-89536-866-8 PRINTED IN U.S.A.

Table of Contents

Editor's Preface

What makes for excellence in parish ministry? That's not easy to say. Clearly, pastoral leadership is the key. But many pastors have provided sterling leadership, only to find unwilling — even hostile or obstreperous — church members crippling every new initiative.

In certain times and places, chemistry combines (and, we believe, the Holy Spirit does the mixing) to provide a happy — no, a *powerful* — result. Before long people in the neighborhood, in nearby congregations, and in district, synod and diocesan offices, begin to say things like, "You know, something remarkable is going on these days at . . ."

In the Fall of 1985, we set about to find twelve good examples of mainline Christian congregations in this country where "something remarkable is going on." We asked assistance from judicatory leaders of a half-dozen denominations to put forth the names of congregations they would most like to see us encourage to provide an essay for a book on Excellence in Ministry. Eleven of the congregations whose stories are in this book were nominated in this way. The twelfth was sought out by the editor, on the strength of its own good reputation.

Read the stories. Be encouraged. Share the good ideas with your parish planners. Do some planning and envisioning. Then, when you're finished, please do us a favor and complete the questionnaire (or you may make your own, or photocopy from the sample in this book). Let us know of a congregation (or two) you would recommend for inclusion in a future volume of similar essays. Who knows? Perhaps *your* congregation ought to be included!

1 | Church Growth

Spirit of Christ Lutheran Church
Ham Lake, Minnesota

Based on positive demographics indicating good population growth in and around Ham Lake and a survey of the homes in the area, the Minnesota South District of the Lutheran Church — Missouri Synod decided to send a pastor to the area to seek to develop a new congregation. On August 1, 1982, Rev. John C. Schildwachter began that assignment. Approximately 3½ years later a flourishing congregation numbering over 500 souls is now serving the area with a rosy future of continued growth forecast for the future. Why this success? Church Growth experts claim that the pastor is critical to growth. That may be, but I would suggest that far more important is the diligent and consistant application of some basic and fundamental axioms that any conscientious pastor could apply with good success. In this short essay I present these axioms with some practical illustrations of their application.

Axiom No. 1 — People can't come to your church unless they know it's there

This axiom may seem so obvious as to be unnecessary to mention. I would contend, however, that if not overlooked completely, in many instances it is not sufficiently considered. At Spirit of Christ we were given added reason to give good attention to making every effort to let people know we were in the community to serve them. The property on which our church building now stands is not particularly well located from the standpoint of high visibility. Our road is not that well traveled, and for architectural and aesthetic reasons, our building is back on the property making it less than obvious to even the relatively few that drive by. We simply had to make a concerted effort to make our presence known.

I would suggest, however, that even those churches located prominently on main thoroughfares can ill afford to take for granted that people know they are there. The following are some of the things we did at Spirit of Christ.

A. We placed **attractive signs** on every major and not-so-major road where people in our area might drive. It's interesting to note how many people came to Spirit of Christ and later joined because of one of our road signs. For those concerned about the cost of such signs, it has been our experience that even on this basis, the investment was good financial stewardship because of the growth of membership that resulted.

B. **Mailings** to all the homes in our area is another device that has served us well. Using a local every-home advertising distribution service, at relatively low cost we can reach every home in reasonable proximity. We try to make our mailings timely and attractive, but most of all, they tell people who may not know, where we are and that we are ready and anxious to serve.

C. **Newcomer visits** are of critical importance because then people are being reached at a time they are more likely to be interested in finding a church home. Visits from Spirit of Christ are made within a week of our awareness of the new family. We always leave a brochure describing the ministry of our church listing times of worship services and Sunday church school and an easy-to-follow map so that people have no trouble finding us.

D. **Newspaper advertising** can also be helpful in making people aware of your presence in the community.

E. **Community surveys** are not nearly as needed if the other items above are employed, but still have a definite place in the outreach of a growing congregation. Callers should give a favorable impression and be trained and well prepared.

Axiom No. 2 — People relate best to people

By far the most frequently-given reason why people join a church is that they were invited by a friend, relative, or some acquaintance. Unfortunately, knowing that doesn't make it happen. To begin with, it takes a vital, Christ-centered church program that makes people enthused and even excited about their church. Then it requires making members aware of the important role they are to play in inviting others. At Spirit of Christ we regularly remind our people of the vital role they have in our continued growth. It also helps to have special happenings that give members "excuses" to specially invite others. Special "Open House" services (described under Axiom No. 4) at Spirit of Christ serve this purpose well. Chancel Dramas, special guest speakers, presentations or musical productions, all serve to give members a special reason to invite their friends, relatives, or other acquaintances.

Axiom No. 3 — Visitors won't continue to come unless they gain a favorable impression from their visit

When a congregation is planted in an area of good growth and/or unchurched homes, and the people in that area know the congregation is there, there are bound to be many who come to visit and "check it out." The critical matter then, is whether or not those visitors return and eventually affiliate with the congregation. Good biblical theology is of course essential, but here I turn your attention rather to those more material aspects of creating a good impression. What we see, hear, taste, smell, and feel will make a decided impression on visitors, and if that impression is unfavorable may cause them to look elsewhere even though the fundamental teaching of the church may be biblical and in keeping with their personal convictions. Here are some examples of what we did at Spirit of Christ to gain that favorable impression.

A. The building itself must look both clean and neat. Few things will "turn off" the visitor faster than, for instance, a dirty restroom with paper towels overflowing the waste basket. Less obvious but also significant (because of the impression it gives) is general neatness. Churches can easily become a resting place for all sorts of items either brought to church or meant to be taken from church. Sunday church school material left behind is the scourge of a neat church. Even kitchen items brought for a potluck meal can be forgotten and left behind. Neatness also applies to those things that normally belong in the church building. Hymn books should be returned to the book rack on the back of the pew or book shelf in orderly fashion. Tract racks also should be kept neatly organized, with dogeared tracts that were looked-at-but-not-taken tossed away. It may not be totally accurate, but there's much truth to the old bromide, "Cleanliness (and neatness) is next to godliness."

B. Landscaping is also important in creating good first impressions. This doesn't require exotic floral arrangements, costly shrubs, or other items that can be expensive to obtain and also expensive and time-consuming to maintain. It *does* require, however, reasonable care of the lawn, trees, and shrubs. It means weeding and watering, but little more than that kind of basic care.

C. Signs and other markings are also to be well maintained. A church I once visited had a sign out front that was poorly done. It was badly weathered and the paint was peeling. I entered that church with a poor impression to begin with. The sign out front, meant to be a welcome, was saying to me, "These people don't think very much of their mission or even the God to whom this church was dedicated."

D. It is also important that visitors are made to feel welcome and wanted. Every congregation should have regular greeters, people who are specially assigned to greet people both before and after the worship service. But more than that, it is important that every member sees it as his/her assignment to stop and talk to visitors. To overcome the problem of people being timid to go up to visitors for fear they may in fact be members, at Spirit of Christ we have all visitors raise their hands to identify themselves at the conclusion of the service. In this way, at least those members close around them are likely to introduce themselves.

E. Prompt and effective follow-up of visitors is also of great importance. This applies to Sunday church school, VCS, youth activities, and other functions, as well as worship. At Spirit of Christ, every visitor is contacted within one week of their visit. A letter is sent to worship visitors on attractive church note paper with a picture of the church on it, thanking them for their visit and inviting them to return. The Pastor also telephones all visitors and asks to visit the home. Even when the home visit doesn't happen because they are not "ready" for a pastoral visitation, a favorable impression is always given.

Axiom No. 4 — People come to church to worship; therefore they expect to be able to relate to the form of worship

The ancient liturgies of the church and their modern variations are rich and beautiful, but the expression and form of much liturgical worship is not something to which many people without that backround can relate — or even understand. Even many Lutherans raised in their church's liturgical traditions don't fully understand the whys and wherefores of the liturgy. The liturgy, then, can be a real stumbling block to church growth and effective outreach. At Spirit of Christ we have tried to come to grips with this problem while at the same time maintaining in general the liturgical character of our worship life. The following are some of the things we have done:

A. Frequent hymn substitutions for various parts of the liturgy not only introduce welcome variation for our members but also tend to make the service more lively and "singable."

B. Explaining parts of the liturgy during the worship service can help members and visitors better to see the beauty and meaning of the service, and it is theologically instructive as well.

C. The worship service is also made more meaningful when the pastor uses his own wording for some of the prayers and other parts of the service.

D. The use of popular hymns not in the Lutheran tradition or hymnbooks can also help people relate to the act of worship taking place.

E. At Spirit of Christ we also have informal "Open House" services on a regular basis. These services are especially designed for the visitor, although members probably appreciate them just as much. In this worship we have a hymn sing with hymns chosen by those in attendance. We also set aside time in the service for a question and answer period. Worshipers are given a list of one hundred or so suggested questions to stimulate the process, but they are free to ask any other questions they choose. These services are *very* well received.

Axiom No. 5 — There's no sense in gaining members only to lose them

It seems at times to this writer that it is less difficult to gain new members than it is to hold them once they're gained. A meaningful, God-pleasing, ministry must not only reach out for the lost sheep, but also nourish and maintain the ninety-nine that are safe in the fold. For the moment, setting aside the importance of biblical nourishment, I turn your attention to those things Spirit of Christ has done in this regard that any congregation could implement as well — and perhaps even better.

A. The most critical time for the new member is those first few weeks. It is in that very beginning when it is usually determined whether or not the membership will "stick." For this reason, at Spirit of Christ every new home is **assigned a sponsor.** The roll of the sponsor, is in general, to help integrate the new member(s) into the congregation. The sponsor is to pray for the new members, make at least one home visit, and make a point of calling attention to various happenings in the congregation to which the new member might best relate. For the home visit, the sponsor(s) receive a packet of items to deliver that are intended to be of interest and informative to the new member. Such things as a copy of the Annual Report and Directory, a schedule of activities for each organization, and a copy of the constitution, are included in the packet.

B. As soon as a person joins Spirit of Christ, a **New Member Notice form** is distributed to every applicable organization or group in the congregation. In this way there is no delay before, for instance, the new woman member is invited to join the women's group or a couple the Fellowship Club. In the same way there is little time lost before the new member will be asked to usher or serve as a greeter or any one of a number of other possibilities to render meaningful service. Bible study groups are also alerted to the new member.

C. Another helpful way of integrating people into the life of the congregation and to feel at home is the regular **meal program** we have here at Spirit of Christ. Periodically, we have potluck dinners to which new members are specially invited. Monthly we have a meal at the church open to all on a cost basis. At $2.25 you couldn't find a better meal — nor better fellowship either!

D. At Spirit of Christ we also want newer members to take an active part in the governance of the congregation. For this reason we have in our by-laws a flexibility as to the size of our various boards. In our short history thus far we have increased the size of our boards every year, not only to better accomplish ever increasing tasks, but also to more readily involve more people without going through the torturous process of rewriting a constitution or by-laws.

*Axiom No. 6. — **The role of the church is to make disciples, not merely members, and that happens only by the Word of God***

It is too easy (what Pastor doesn't know!) to get caught up in a numbers game and simply strive to increase the size of the membership list. Needless to say, however, this is not the role of the church. Her marching orders are abundantly clear. "Therefore go and make disciples of all nations, baptizing them in the name of the Father and of the Son and of the Holy Spirit, and teaching them to obey everything I have commanded you." (Matthew 28:19-20a NIV) In a word, we are here to win souls for Christ, to bring people into a faith relationship with him. No contrivance or program of the church can make this happen. This is the work of the Holy Spirit, who in turn works through the Word of God. It is, then, the task of the church to present that Word in winning and winsome fashion, both to members and prospective members. Striving to be faithful to its mandate, at Spirit of Christ we do all in our power to bring that Word to bear.

A. All **preaching** is rooted and grounded in the Word. Law and Gospel are our steady diet. That's not to say the message is to be simply a theological regurgitation of theological fact.

On the contrary, we seek to relate that Word to the lives of people so that by that Word they may come to know or increase in the joy of their salvation. Sunday church school, Bible classes, VCS, confirmation classes, are all aimed toward that central goal.

B. Specifically designed for the prospective member, although quite often members also attend, is our **Adult Inquirer's Class.** These classes meet nine times and are designed to cover the basics of the biblical faith. There are seldom more than fifteen in a class and open discussion and inquiry is encouraged. Enrollees are in no way made to feel obligated to join the congregation. These classes not only serve to bring the Word of God to bear in the lives of those who attend, they also make people feel more comfortable with the teaching of the church. Long-supressed doubt and questions can be openly addressed and denominational differences can be aired in a non-threatening and loving environment. Good things happen in Adult Inquirer Classes.

C. In general, from the church brochure briefly stating our basic faith to the worship services and Bible Classes or Bible study that is also often part of our various organizations and other groups, **the Word of Scripture is central** at Spirit of Christ Lutheran Church. After all, "How can they believe in the One of whom they haven't heard?" (Romans 10:14)

Many books have been written on the subject of Church Growth in recent years. Every professional worker in the church should become informed on this subject and benefit by the sound research and conclusions drawn in these books. My ministry has profited by them. But a diligent and consistant application of just the "axioms" in this essay will bring some significant results.

Soli Deo Gloria

— ***John C. Schildwachter***

Ideas which this chapter sparks for possible application in our congregation:

Resources we already have in our congregation which could facilitate such a ministry thrust:

People in our congregation who should read this chapter — and who may be good candidates for a task force:

2 | Community Outreach Through Early Childhood Education

Saint John's Lutheran Church
Bakersfield, California

Early Childhood Education, or ECE, has been around for a few years. Some of the more familiar pioneers were the Headstart programs aimed at low income areas and the Montessori schools that seemed directed more toward the affluent households. Day-care centers were emerging at the end of World War II. Preschools, as we know them today, seem to be a consolidation of all three, depending on the individual focus of the sponsoring agency. In recent years there has been a marked increase in franchise child care centers. The Lutheran Church-Missouri Synod began to see mission potential in the 1960s. During the following decade more and more churches began to use their Sunday church school facilities to accomodate the child care needs of their members, as well as their communities.

It was during the early 1970s that I first became involved. I might add that my involvement was not totally "my" intention, but rather something that began to happen around me and I responded to the need. Since that time I have been instrumental in the establishment of several child care centers. The first was in suburban Minneapolis and the most recent in Bakersfield, California. I will be focusing my attention on the Christian Children's Center in Bakersfield.

Saint John's is the mother Lutheran Church of Bakersfield. Organized in the early 1900s, she has given birth to several daughter congregations. Saint John's has relocated three times.

The most recent move in 1967 brought her to the southwest edge of one of the fastest growing cities in the San Joaquin Valley. When my family and I arrived in December of 1976, construction on a new youth-education building was just beginning. The 6500 square foot classroom and youth center was a much-needed addition to the congregation of 500-plus members who were being equipped and trained to take their personal ministries out into the community. Pastor Norb Oesch had been with them for just over a year when he encouraged the congregation to add a full-time minister of education and youth. He had been here almost two years when I arrived in December of 1976.

The first several months of my tenure were devoted to getting acquainted and assessing needs. The average age of the congregation was approximately forty-five and there was a fairly active youth group. The Sunday church school, however, had a total enrollment of fifty children between the ages of four and thirteen. Baptisms were uncommon!

As the new building was nearing completion, I felt an intense need to see a program organized that would utilize this prime space. My time was spent with high school-aged youth, but my concentration was on the obvious void of young families and young children.

I talked at length with Pastor Oesch and other key people about the potential of a preschool. They were encouraging and suggested I begin the process of determining if it was feasible. The Board of Education was supportive and listened as I shared my previous experiences with Early Childhood Education.

During the spring of 1977 the building was dedicated and I had my first meeting with the Early Childhood Education state licensing agent. Since each state is different, she was extremely helpful in supplying me with the necessary handbook and paperwork that I needed for California.

The building, not designed for preschool-aged children, would be acceptable with a few minor alterations in the restrooms. My next step was to determine what kind of interest there was from within the congregation. I made phone calls, set out questionnaires, and talked to anyone who would listen. I finally had enough interested people to form a committee. I did not want it to be "my" preschool; rather, it was to be ours as a congregation.

The committee talked for hours about the type of program they wanted to see offered. Should it be a preschool, a day-care center, a parent co-op, or what? Where would we get our teachers? What would we pay them? How much should tuition be? What about equipment and other supplies?

At this time the questions seemed endless. But as they were asked, we seemed always to find acceptable answers. During the summer of 1977 I made the first presentation to a voter's meeting. Much to my surprise they listened and asked many of the same questions that had already been asked in the Board of Education and the committee. Our timing was good because we were not yet ready to open our doors, we also did not yet have answers for all of their questions. They asked that we re-open the discussion in the fall for further consideration.

At this point we had not spent any money, nor did we have any to spend. We were, however, approaching the time that, if we were serious, we needed access to some funds for initial expenses. One young mother suggested that all we needed was a couple boxes of crayons, some scissors, glue, and construction paper! That might have done it, but it was not the kind of program that I envisioned us having. Our greatest need was a fenced playground with some toys with which the children could play.

Enthusiasm was growing from within the committee as we crossed one hurdle after another. It spread to other families with young children. Closets were going to be cleaned and outgrown toys would be donated if we needed them.

As the day approached for our presentation to the congregation, we felt ready. Our purpose, objectives, and motivation were clear. We had tentative commitment from some parents and we felt that our tuition rates would cover our costs.

The major stumbling block was the fence — $487.00 for materials.

The meeting was opened after the end of the late worship service. The attendance was light and most of the men looked as if they would much rather have been home eating lunch and watching the Rams play Dallas. Some of those same thoughts went through my mind as well. As the chairman of the congregation called me to the front to make my presentation and subsequent proposal, I felt as if time had stopped. In my mind I felt confident that what we were attempting to do was a good thing. The presentation went smoothly and I was able to answer the questions satisfactorily. The only unanswered question concerned the money for the fence. The silence was deafening. Finally, from the back of the room, came a raspy voice: "If the only thing holding us back is a fence, I'll buy it! And besides that, I think it's a good idea." The chairman called for a vote. It was unanimous. (At least, I *think* it was! I was so estatic I don't remember.) The only stipulation was that the program had to be self-supporting or we would have to close it down. That was fair!

That decision to begin was not the most important to be made in the history of the congregation. The impact that it would have in the next six to eight years would be one of great significance, however. On Monday my task was to get the wheels turning, and turn they did. Enrollment forms, medical forms, and all of the other forms were sent out to the prospective students' homes. We desperately needed the $10.00 registration fee so that we could start to order supplies. We had established February 1, 1978, as our opening day. There was nothing magic about the date. We simply felt that would allow us time enough to get things ready.(You can open a preschool anytime during the year; September isn't the only acceptable date. In fact, opening mid-year has some advantages insofar as you have some time to make some mistakes and get them corrected before the fall term.)

On Halloween night, a tragedy struck one of our families.

Their three-year-old daughter was struck and killed by a hit-and-run driver. It was one of those senseless things that always seem to go unanswered. But our Lord has a way of turning tragedies into miracles. This family had received some memorial money, given in remembrance, and they wanted it spent on something for children. I asked if a fence might qualify, especially for our preschool. They not only agreed, but the father volunteered to put it up!

On February 1 we had fourteen children enrolled. Eight would come on Monday, Wednesday and Friday and six on Tuesdays and Thursdays. The numbers weren't what I had hoped for, but we were open for business. The Christian Children's Center was a reality. Our half-day teacher and director was as excited as was I to greet the children and their parents on those opening days. As the weeks passed we managed to add a few more children. We still were not covering all of our expenses, but we weren't going into the red.

The Board of Education had assured me that they would finance us during the interim. That sounded good, and yet it wasn't a blank check either. We had to be responsible. The children had a good time and our message was that "we care for them in a way that Jesus cares for us." We ended that term in June several hundred dollars in the red, but thousands of dollars smarter. We had pre-registered for the fall and were nearly full. We did some advertising — as much as we could afford. Our best recruiters were our students and their satisfied parents. In the fall of 1978 we started a waiting list that grew to the point of requiring adding another teacher. That waiting list grew to another and another and another. Our program grew and grew and still grows.

In our first class, seventy-five percent of the children were mambers of the congregation. That number has dropped steadily since. Today Early Childhood Education has expanded to include two different campuses and an enrollment of over 250 children. It also includes the beginning of an elementary school. In September we will have over 150 children in Kindergarten through grade five. Our original fourteen children have grown to be a staff of twenty-eight full- and part-time teachers.

How has this effected the growth of the church? Since that first day in February of 1978, over 500 people have become members as a direct result of the preschool and elementary school. Our Sunday church school boasts an enrollment of nearly 300. Vacation church school participation has grown from 120 to nearly 500. We have nearly forty baptisms a year. Most are infants. The average age of the congregation is somewhere in the early twenties.

The strategy involved in this kind of growth is relatively simple. We know that the most precious treasure parents have in this world are their children. We give them our best, which is our genuine love and care. Our teachers are our first line of the ministry team and we are certain they are aware of that. Each child is special and that is constantly being instilled in their minds.

More than eighty percent of the children are not members of our church when the school year begins. Of that eighty percent, half will be without a church home. Our strategy for changing those numbers is deliberate. As the school year begins, we are certain that the parents realize our school is a Christian school — we teach, "Jesus, our Lord and Savior." We are not attempting to make them Lutheran, but encouraging them to be involved with a church. We do not flood their mailboxes with church correspondence. Instead, we send a casual invitation to attend the pastor's class if they are interested in knowing more about the Lutheran faith. We will get a few takers in September, but not many. When the school term begins, so do our weekly chapel services for the children. Our ministerial staff takes turns leading these and the children get to know who these people are. During the fall we will have several "open houses" and other non-threatening fellowship activities on campus. Most of the unchurched are frightened to enter the sanctuary, so we direct their attention to the *whole* campus. In mid-November we begin to prepare the children to sing in a Thanksgiving Eve service. This is probably the least threatening of any service, and the fact that the children will be singing helps to get a good response. The service is designed for those people who have little church experience. It is a good service and they walk away feeling comfortable. No one tried to "save" them; we simply were able to celebrate together. When the service is over, the ministerial staff greet the children, or in some cases, the children greet us, which allows us the opportunity of meeting their parents. Also, while they are here, they sign our guest register and on the following Monday, a postcard from the pastor acknowledges their presence.

As the Christmas season gets closer, we send home a little brochure that outlines our special Christmas services and invites them to join us. Many of them do attend. Again, we are focusing on the people who do not have a tradition of worshiping.

In January, they will receive a formal invitation to attend the pastor's class along with some words of encouragement from the children's teachers. The trust relationships that have developed between parent and teacher since September is becoming quite strong. More parents now respond.

The congregation has taken education seriously. This provides for a variety of opportunities for adults to be involved. Our school parents are invited to participate whenever they can. These contacts have helped to build many lasting friendships, and have strengthened the bond between church and community. We realize that not everyone is going to respond in the same way and that we are not going to be able to touch the lives of every person who crosses our threshold. We do know, however, that the love we share in the morning with the children will be shared by them with others later in the day.

A word of caution is in order. This kind of outreach ministry may or may not meet your needs. It requires hard work and patience. There will be some suffering involved. Not everyone will share the same vision. What was once an available space will be occupied. And "who are all of the *new* people?"

will be a common refrain. But if we take seriously God's call, to "go to all nations," (in this case the nations come to you), it is a tremendous opportunity to reach out and care for people.

—Stanley G. Smidt

Ideas which this chapter sparks for possible application in our congregation:

Resources we already have in our congregation which could facilitate such a ministry thrust:

People in our congregation who should read this chapter -- and who may be good candidates for a task force:

3 | Dollar Stewardship

Cross United Church of Christ
Berne, Indiana

A plant responds to its environment. If the seed is good, if it is planted in fertile soil, if it receives proper nourishment, if it is not felled by evil circumstances, it will grow into a healthy plant bearing good fruit. The same is true for human beings; the same is true for collections of human beings called congregations.

The seed from which grew the Cross United Church of Christ was planted in good soil. This area of northeast Indiana, fertile and productive, was settled by people who had been farmers in the "Old Country" (in our area, from Switzerland), who saw God at work in their occupation. The environment in the town of Berne, Indiana, had been established by a devout group of Mennonites when our German Reformed Church congregation was organized. In such an environment Cross Church was nourished, fiercely loyal to its Zwinglian heritage. The people brought with them a respect for hard labor and an abhorrence for debt. To be able to say "I don't owe anyone anything!" was considered a mark of good character. If a debt was an absolute necessity (for a farm, a home, later a car if needed for work, or an education), there was a plan for payment.

Which debts, if a person had any, were to be paid first? High on the list of priorities was the obligation to the church. How deeply entrenched this feeling was in one member — a man of meager means with a family to support — is illustrated by the following story:

One day the member bought himself a much needed suit.

Then he became a troubled man. He had pledged a certain amount as his apportionment to the church, but now, having bought the suit, he was beset by doubts as to whether he could meet his obligations. The result was that he took his suit back to the store, reclaimed his money, and paid his apportionment.

Deeply dedicated ministers fostered this spirit of giving. Reverend Bechtold Ruf, who pastored the Reformed church some seventy-five years ago, felt that the needy should not have to call attention to their needs, but that congregations should be aware of them and give so that there would be money in reserve when needed.

"Papa" Ruf addressed the children of the congregation one day in Sunday School. "Here is a little box," he said. "Now I think it would be very fine if, when you have a birthday, you'd bring a penny for each year you have lived and drop those pennies into this box. Then you, too, will have given money for the poor children."

At each home, previous to departure for Sunday church school, Father gave each child a penny for the offering plate. So early the habit of giving was passed from one generation to another. It was ingrained in the minds of the congregation.

I'm no good at asking for anything for myself," said "Papa" Ruf, "but I can beg for others." In this spirit he started the Dorcas Sewing Society and the Ladies' Aid.

Years rolled on. Methods of bringing in money might change from one generation to another but not the determination to bring it in. And always there was strong emphasis on mission work.

Picture the years of the 20s and 30s. On a certain Sunday night Cross Church is filled to capacity. Not a seat is left empty in the church; people are standing — people from our church, neighboring churches, and for miles around. What's going on? The Girl's Guild is giving a play. It has become an annual affair. All girls in the Guild have a part in its production; actors for male parts are drafted from men in the congregation. The play has a missionary message, the most powerful, perhaps, having been presented in the play "The Pill Box." Many hours have gone into preparation for the play's presentation. The appreciation of the audience and the well-filled offering plates make it all worthwhile.

The play is a part of the Thankoffering time. Thankoffering boxes have been gathered in the morning worship service, boxes whose contents are symbols of gratitude for blessings received and of a desire to share with "the least of these." Did Johnny recover from his illness? Yes. A coin is dropped into the box. Did Mary pass her history test? Yes. Into the box goes another thankoffering. The sum total of the play offerings and box offerings is gratifying. It will do much good in the Kingdom.

Time marched on. There were tithers. There were those who gave generously for specific pet projects, secretly or openly, which helped swell the amount in the treasury. Some members used envelopes for their weekly offerings while others preferred to give in lump sums now and then. Through the year, whatever the method, the generous spirit behind the donations persisted.

Let us focus now on the 70s and 80s. Another event has sprung up. It is called the Annual Youth Auction. But make no mistake: the whole congregation, young and old, has been preparing for it for months. Many persons have put their particular talents to work for the event: sewing, quilting, baking, carpentering, painting and repairing usable items, constructing unique articles appealing to the nostalgia in us.

An auction? Yes. But it is much, much more than that. It is a concerted effort to raise money for specific mission projects such as supplying a medical missionary with necessary instruments, digging a well in Togo, building houses for the poor, counseling alcoholics.

The auction is also a social event for the whole community. Once held in the country at the auctioneer's home and now in the Berne park under a tent, the site is surrounded many-deep by cars. Amish buggies stand behind patient horses tied to hitching racks.

The event is yet more: it is a chicken barbecue. Long before 4:00 p.m. (starting time to eat) the air is filled with the tantalizing aroma of barbecuing chicken and smoke rising from the grills. Under the tent a line of people is forming before the food is on display. Behind the serving table are the congregation's youth, ready to dish out chicken, carrot sticks, baked beans, potato chips, lemonade or coffee. The auction will have started before the last customers have finished eating.

Meanwhile, you are struck with the number of strangers present — mostly young men, but also a few young women. Something is singularly different about some of them: a few wear western hats; one lady wears a barn-dance costume; several appear ill at ease, restless. They are the student auctioneers from the Reppert Auctioneering School. They are like young birds trying out their inexperienced voices. This evening they will appear before the assembled crowd and be asked to sell the accumulated goods contributed by the congregation. Some of the would-be auctioneers swing into action with confidence, in control of the situation; a very few try valiantly to sell an article and sink into helpless confusion. The crowd sympathizes, and the article is always sold. Selling goes on smoothly for the most part. People know the purpose of the occasion. They know why they are there: they have come to buy, often at prices far beyond the real value of the item being sold.

A pan of homemade rolls is exhibited. The auctioneer peers at the name of the baker taped on the wrap and announces it. The name arouses instant interest — there are some mighty fine cooks in our church. "What am I bid for these fine looking rolls?" cries the auctioneer. "Five dollars? Who'll give six?" urges the auctioneer. A lifted hand waves. (At the grocery store the rolls might sell for $1.15.)

"I have six, nowsixwho'llgivesevengiveseven?" the auctioneer's voice rolls on.

"Yes!" shouts a student auctioneer as his eyes comb the assembly to spot the bidders.

"Seven dollars. Now eight, now eight." The contest is narrowed to two bidders. Enough is enough, even for good causes; one person admits defeat. Baked goods sell well; the women have years ago built up a reputation. Pies sell well, especially ground cherry pies. One has been known to sell for $130. A pound of candy sold for $50; about one-half pound of yellow popcorn, $35.

A little wave of excitement spills over the assembly as the auctioneer in charge summons the pastor of the church to the front and places the responsibility of sales of the next few articles into his hands. The minister rises gallantly to the occasion: he comes through triumphantly.

The auction goes on for several hours. The results put smiles on the faces of the youth. In 1985 nearly $10,000 was raised — *all for mission causes at home and abroad!*.

Giving is spurred on by contact with the missionaries and agencies by whom the proceeds realized will be used. A visit to our church by a missionary on furlough or an agency representative reminds — *encourages* — us to keep on giving. Always we remember: what we give

We give Thee but Thine own,
Whate'er the gift may be.
All that we have is Thine alone,
A trust, O Lord, from Thee.

— *Helen Macklin*

Ideas which this chapter sparks for possible application in our congregation:

Resources we already have in our congregation which could facilitate such a ministry thrust:

People in our congregation who should read this chapter — and who may be good candidates for a task force:

4 | Evangelism

Trinity Lutheran Church
Atchison, Kansas

"Evangelism potential?" This question was one of many on the standard call document which Pastor Robert Ziegler received from Trinity Lutheran Church, Atchison, Kansas, in July, 1969. The answer the congregation gave at that time was: "Very little — the town is well-churched." When asked today about evangelism potential, members of Trinity respond with enthusiasm: "Great! The fields are white unto harvest. There are hundreds and hundreds of people in our town and community who are yet to be won for Christ." What has brought about the change in attitude? A dynamic program of evangelism and outreach.

Atchison, Kansas has a population of approximately 11,000. Since 1969 it has lost well over a thousand people and several hundred jobs. Yet in this same period Trinity has received through adult confirmation, 456 people. The congregation has grown from 527 communicants and 793 souls to 846 communicants and 1135 souls. Average Sunday worship attendance has grown from 308 to 532. Enrollment in the Christian Day School has grown from 108 to 206. Enrollment in Sunday church school and adult Bible classes has grown from 211 to 513. Budget giving has grown from $65,000 to $328,000. The staff has grown. All of this has come gradually through much work, lots of prayer, and continued calling and visiting. Most growing churches are in areas of growing population. What makes the story of Trinity, Atchison, unique, is that it is in an area of declining population.

In the beginning there was nothing spectacular. The spirit of the congregation was low. Its self-esteem was at rock-bottom. There were many problems. Pastor Ziegler spent hours and hours calling in the homes of the members, getting to know them, encouraging them, gaining their respect and confidence. Faithfully, he took care of the pastoral needs of the people. Having been raised in an alcoholic home, he worked and counseled especially in this area of need. He spent much time preparing sermons, lessons for Adult Bible Class, and devotions for meetings. Through all of these he emphasized the Great Commission, the meaning of discipleship, the command of Christ to win souls and make disciples, the purpose for local congregations, the vision of growth that Christ sets before his people. In the beginning years, the pastor personally called on every person who visited a worship service and twice a year, visited and telephoned in order to gather people into adult instruction classes.

A few new people joined the congregation. The visiting, preaching, and teaching began to bear fruit. A new spirit began to develop. People began to ask if they could help. An Evangelism Committee was formed. Committee members began making "welcome calls" to visitors. Soon the committee members were asking for some kind of learning experience which would enable them to really witness and talk about Jesus and their faith in him. Trinity is an old congregation, founded in 1866. Looking back, Pastor Ziegler believes that the four years, 1969-1974, were "getting ready" years. Without them, what was later to happen would not have happened.

In January, 1974, Pastor Ziegler attended a seminar led by the Reverend Donald Abdon of Parish Leadership Seminars, Indianapolis, Indiana. At that seminar Pastor Ziegler learned of Abdon's sixteen-week Adult Inquirer Class. It was designed as a review of basic Christian teaching, to get people back into the Bible, and to answer the religious, biblical questions adults are asking. In the Fall of 1974, the Adult Inquirer Class became a vital part of the teaching and equipping ministry of

Trinity. Since then the pastor has taught this course twice every year, beginning on the last Sunday of January and the last Sunday of August. Classes are held on Sunday afternoons from 4:00 to 6:00 p.m. Child care is provided. Since its inception over 1,000 people have completed the course. This course, added to the four years of ground work, sparked the growth momentum.

In the Spring of 1975, James Kennedy's *Evangelism Explosion* was begun. The training was conducted just as Dr. Kennedy outlines it. Members were asked to commit themselves to sixteen weeks of training and calling every Monday evening from 6:30 to 10:30 p.m. This training was to take priority over all else. Strict discipline and faithfulness were asked. This program continues to be the backbone of Trinity's evangelism program. Some 130 persons have now been trained through this method of evangelism.

Teams of two or three persons go calling each Monday evening. Trainers and trainees arrive at 6:30 p.m. The evening begins with singing, scriptural devotion, and prayer. From 7:00 to 7:30 p.m. trainees recite memory work to their trainers. From 7:30 to 9:00 p.m. the teams go calling. At 9:00 the teams return to the church to make out reports of their calls and write cards to those on whom they have called, thanking them for their hospitality and praying God's blessings on them. From 9:30 to 10:00 p.m., team members attend a class of instruction. There are different classes for trainees, support people, and trainers. From 10:00 to 10:30 p.m. verbal reports of all calls are made to the leader in the presence of the whole group. This is designed to be a learning experience for new as well as experienced callers. At 10:30 p.m. the evening is closed with circle prayer, two persons plus the pastor praying individually for all those called on during the evening.

In Evangelism Explosion, homes are visited several times. After the Gospel has been presented, teams return in the weeks following to share a two-lesson Bible study entitled, "Your Decision", produced by the Navigators. Those called upon are placed on the congregational mailing list. Contact is maintained even if the person does not immediately come to the worship services. At VCS time, teams take enrollment blanks to all families with children. Before each Adult Inquirer Class begins, teams take enrollment forms to all homes previously visited. At Christmas and Easter hundreds of invitations to worship are sent to all homes contacted through the year. Also, if there is a special musical program, invitations are taken by teams to homes they have previously visited. Contact is maintained as long as the home is receptive and the family has not joined another church.

Names of people to be called on come from many sources. Each new member is asked for the names of unchurched friends and relatives. From time to time forms for listing unchurched neighbors, co-workers, etc., are placed in the Sunday bulletin. Newcomers to the community are visited. Unchurched parents of children in the Christian Day School, Vacation church school, church school, scouting programs, are visited. As small as our town is, we have never wanted for names of people on whom to call.

In 1980 high school youth teams were added to the program. After youth are trained on regular adult teams they are formed into youth teams to call on other youth. In January of 1986 child evangelism was added. Young people in the seventh and eighth grades commit themselves to four weeks of training and go out with adult trainers to visit and present the Gospel to children of the first and second grade level. The purpose of these programs is both immediate and long-term, bringing the Gospel *now* and laying a foundation for *future* work in evangelism.

Reception to our calling teams in the community has been excellent. Seldom have visitors been denied entrance.

Prayer is vital to the program. Each person involved in the program has a prayer partner. Each week the program's prayer chairman brings prayer partners to the church during the time the callers are out calling, praying for them as they make their calls. During the reporting period, 10:00 to 10:30 p.m., these prayer partners report on prayers answered that evening. A special Prayer and Praise Service is held on the first Friday evening of each month. Petitions are brought to the Lord for the congregation's evangelism program, for unchurched spouses, relatives, and friends of members, and for church growth in general. Evangelism and growth are prayed for before the altar in Sunday services.

On the Sunday before every training cycle, a congregational potluck dinner is held. New trainees are introduced and receive their study material. Trainers and support people are recognized. Usually a film on evangelism or church growth is shown. Testimonies about what Evangelism Explosion has meant to them are given by callers. People who have completed training are "pinned" during one of the services on Sunday morning. In these ways the work of evangelism is kept continually before the congregation.

In the summer of 1983, Mr. Jerry Bisping joined the staff of Trinity as its first full-time Director of Evangelism. As D.E., Mr. Bisping is responsible not only for evangelism, but also for the incorporation of new members into the life of the congregation and for the fellowship activities of the congregation. Jerry has led the congregation through a church growth study process and is presently teaching Win Arn's "The Master's Plan," a class on spiritual gifts, and Leighton Ford's course, "Good News Is For Sharing." He has also conducted several Saturday workshops on witnessing.

There are three services in the Sunday worship schedule of Trinity, 8:00, 10:30 a.m., and 6:30 p.m The 6:30 p.m. service has been an aid to the evangelism program. Unchurched people are not accustomed to getting up early on Sunday mornings for worship. Since our Adult Inquirer Class is from 4:00 to 6:00 p.m., many enrolled in it stay for worship at 6:30. There has been steady growth in the number of people at this service. However, since fewer people do attend it than the morning services, it is advertised as a service for those who like a "small church" atmosphere.

With evangelism there must also be edification. Through the years Trinity has developed a fine program of adult education. There are three Sunday morning adult Bible classes with an enrollment of some 280. A new class which meets at 5:15 p.m. was recently started for those who attend the 6:30 service. In 1978 the congregation began using the Bethel Bible Series. In 1983, what is called the T.E.A.M. Program (Teaching and Equipping Adults for Ministry) was started. This program consists of several classes which are taught on Tuesday evenings in seven-week sessions. Three such seven-week sessions are held each year. Classes in the areas of Bible study, ministry skills, and family living are offered. Also, several home Bible study groups meet each week. Bible study is constantly encouraged and prayed for in worship services.

An active evangelism program brings to light the various hurting needs of people. In 1979, Trinity established its H.E.L.P. Program. H.E.L.P. stands for "Here's Encouragement, Love, and Power". It is a family counseling program with special concentration on the problems connected with alcoholism. It is staffed by Ellen Hawk, a certified alcoholism counselor. Many people have been drawn to Trinity and helped through this program. To minister to the pastoral needs of the growing numbers of people, the congregation entered the Stephen Ministry Program in 1986.

Music is also an important ministry in a growing, evangelism minded church. Trinity's Director of Christian Education, Mike Peitsch, is developing this area of ministry. He is also in charge of Vacation church school which is vigorously promoted because of its evangelism potential. The position of Director of Christian Education was added to the staff in 1980.

Changes have been made in the area of worship. So that the visitor may immediately participate in the worship service, the hymnal is being used less; the service has become more informal; less liturgy is being used; and service guides are being printed. Careful attention is given to the choosing of hymns that are positive, inspiring, and uplifting. Child care is available for all services. Since the worship service is the church's "front window", much attention is given to its being attractive and meaningful. Doormen stand outside and open the doors and greet all who come to worship. Friendliness and warmth are constantly encouraged and stressed.

Another avenue of evangelism is Trinity's Christian Day School. Staffed by six teachers, the school charges no tuition for either member or non-member children. Through the years many children and their parents have come to know the Savior through the school.

Space soon becomes a problem for a growing church. To help solve the problem at Trinity, three mobile classrooms are now being used, and two residential homes have been purchased and are being used. Three homes have been purchased and torn down to provide parking space. A new building with classrooms, gym, and fellowship area is on the drawing boards.

None of what has been described above would be possible without scores of dedicated, hard-working, generous laymen and laywomen. Evangelism programs and growing churches are not built overnight. They come from years of disciplined work and effort. Staff longevity and stability are tremendously important. Growth comes where there is continuity in leadership and vision. Undergird all of this with fervent and continued prayer, and growth can come even to old established congregations in communities which are declining in population.

— Robert M. Ziegler

Ideas which this chapter sparks for possible application in our congregation:

Resources we already have in our congregation which could facilitate such a ministry thrust:

People in our congregation who should read this chapter — and who may be good candidates for a task force:

5 Ministry to Refugees

Grace Episcopal Church
Sheboygan, Wisconsin

In his "Ballad of East and West," Rudyard Kipling wrote, "Oh, East is East and West is West, and never the twain shall meet, till earth and sky stand presently at God's great judgment seat . . ." But those of us who have been involved in resettling great numbers of Southeast Asians believe the reverse to be true. The cultures shall indeed meet, sometimes on a collision course, but often in complement one to the other.

It was just over five years ago that a handful of Indochinese refugees began appearing on the streets of the sleepy Midwestern town of Sheboygan, Wisconsin. This semi-rural community is located just sixty miles north of Milwaukee, and has provided solace for lake weary travelers since the early fur trading days of the 1830s.

Sheboygan, once the "gem of Lake Michigan," is situated on the mouth of the Sheboygan River where it occupies a natural harbor, a welcome respite from the lake sometimes-turbulent. As late as 1910, lake clippers, paddlewheelers, and engine-powered sailboats anchored in the Sheboygan harbor, or were launched into the "great deep" by one of the eight shipyards in the area. Over the past 130 years, immigrant groups landed on these shores to start a new life in the "land that goes down to the sea."

The early Dutch residents of the county refused to build too near the lake, so their communities were founded inland. During the summer months the farm families would tent-camp along the sprawling shores of Lake Michigan to enjoy the lake breezes, and "take the cure" (if that were indeed possible) through the freshness of the fog-shrouded mornings, or even to walk the great distance to that "great leviathan" over acres of scorching beach.

The Dutch were followed by the "Volga Germans," who had heard of the prosperity in this land, and specifically of the factory jobs in Sheboygan. Even Tamburiza music filled the air on summer evenings as immigrants arrived from Slovenia and Croatia. They, too, sought positions and a new life in this land of plenty. Greeks from the shores of the Adriatic arrived and promptly founded the first Greek Orthodox parish north of Chicago. They were able to procure jobs and establish grocery stores, to the delight of community members.

Sheboygan had hardly noticed the influx of these European immigrants as they blended into the local scene of fishing and boating, where great smokestacks belched a prosperous welcome to newcomers.

The community, now in the throes of change, has struggled with its factories, its work force, its downtown, attempting to address a kind of renewal — to provide continuing jobs in the "new age" of computer mania. An expansive walking plaza, surrounded by historic buildings — some with face lifts, others badly in need of repair — has replaced the streets of yesterday. The mood has not been good for such a change.

It was into such a culture, dominated by Northern European influence, pampered by the tradition of numerous factory jobs, that our newest ethnic group arrived. These refugees were noted immediately. They were not the clones of continental lookalikes, nor were they mistaken for the dark-skinned Greeks from the isles. The earliest comments heard from those on park benches were, "They must be Vietnamese, or perhaps they're just visiting!" The "visits" continued, but many of the residents tended to ignore the fact that more and more Asians were arriving on the scene. Suddenly a great need became evident as children were observed walking about in "tennies" at thirty below zero with an accumulation of two feet of snow. Stories were even circulating that "they" were building bonfires in the middle of their apartment floors to keep warm.

It was at this time that Grace Church became involved. Armed with some sketchy facts about Southeast Asians, parishioners began to make calls in the fast-forming ghetto on the plaza. They discovered that fourteen families were living in substandard housing above the shops.

As we entered the hallways we were struck with the curious odors emitting from the apartments. As calls were made on one family, other doors would pop open and more Asian eyes would peek at the four somewhat confused Anglos — a priest, an adult woman and her two adolescent children. These early days were frightening because there was always the immediate problem of communication — although inevitably someone would happen on the scene who could speak enough English to help us communicate.

Slowly it became possible to piece together the facts: our newest residents were from Laos; they were mountain people called Hmong (free people); and their only contact with a modern society had been their assistance of the Central Intelligence Agency during Vietnam. Under the leadership of General Vang Pao, a modern-day Khan, this "new" golden horde fought against the prowess of the Viet Cong. These brave new citizens had come from a slash-and-burn society. Indeed, they had moved from valley to valley in the mountains of Laos as they exhausted the use of the land. Formed in small villages, they resided in long houses akin to the native American domiciles. After the fall of Saigon they became a hunted people, and were forced to descend from their mountains and to attempt forging the Mekong River.

Along with the Hmong tribesman came their culture, their haute cuisine, and their art forms — including numerous pieces of Pa ndau (pronounced pan dow), examples of reverse applique, and their story cloths depicting all aspects of their former life in the mountains.

The first Hmong families had arrived in the late 1970s. Now we were experiencing a landslide of family reunification. The local training school, Lakeshore Technical Institute, was flooded with refugees who were enrolling in ESL (English as a Second Language) classes. But there were many who fell between the cracks — nursing mothers, older relatives, all members of an "extended family." It was obvious that Grace Church must rise to the occasion. After talking with the clan leaders, it was possible to offer our parish center facility for Laubach Literacy classes, Western culture classes, health classes, and as a "community center." Soon it was even possible on any given weekday to observe between thirty and forty Hmong people of all ages busily learning the ways of this new land and culture.

On one occasion a middle-aged Hmong lady of my acquaintance stood at my office door and, in halting English, said, "Mother — no — Father, may we come to your parish?" And so it started. One by one, family after family arrived to participate in our high mass on Sunday mornings. We were cautious not to exact any recompense for our contributions toward the Hmong Community. We gave freely and expected nothing in return but an occasional smiling face. Our clothing drives and furniture round-ups had no strings attached. Although adults and young people alike became involved with the community, never did they expect the Hmong to leave their native religion, which was in most cases animism.

Early in January of 1981 an instruction class was started for Indochinese people. The basic tenets of the Episcopal Church were dealt with through the kind assistance of several Hmong interpreters. Later that season we asked our new Indochinese friends what they actually expected from us — whether they were satisfied coming to the altar for a blessing, or whether they wanted to receive Christ's Body and Blood. Their response: "We want the real thing."

After months of preparation, the first Hmong mass Baptism was held, at which time thirty-nine people participated in the Sacrament of Christian initiation. They spent some time choosing "strange new names," and were baptized with their Christian name and their Hmong name. All ages, from heads of households to babes in arms, were brought to the font; the entire congregation acted as godparents. The instruction classes continued, and at the Easter Vigil Mass of 1983 sixty-five Hmong tribesmen made the journey, preceded by the Light of Christ, to the font. Once again the Christian names were chosen, the sponsors gathered, candles lighted, water poured and heads made greasy with the sacred oil of Chrism.

It had been a long way from the highlands of Laos, across the Mekong, and through the "holding camps" of Thailand. But now change permeated the air with its fragrance: a new country, a new life style, a new religion.

As a result of those first baptisms, the Episcopal Indochinese Society was formed to nourish the faith of the new brothers and sisters. Each family was given a crucifix for their home. The Society met weekly for instruction on the Sunday Sripture propers, for prayer, and of course for the Eucharist. Quarterly dinners were held to encourage the ongoing relationship between Hmong and American parishioners. In the Spring of 1982 an Indochinese Commission was established to further encourage sponsorship, catechesis, and to prepare Anglo parishes for the influx of Asian parishioners. This commission began sponsoring a refugee Sunday in the diocese, and the Indochinese games, which endeavor to unite Episcopalian refugees with a common belief and a common interest. A Hmong/Lao Mass is celebrated, cuisine prepared (one year there were five cultures represented at the Liturgy and in the culinary efforts), and a gigantic soccer game is played, with athletic activities also for the smaller children. The commission has put together a "how-to" sponsorship kit, the Indochinese Archives (which contain religious and secular hints on available service in the State of Wisconsin), and at the present time are working on a Hmong catechism.

After the Hmong had been on the parish scene for two

years, a number of Cambodian refugees filtered into the Sheboygan area. Nearly thirty of them joined the parish. Their background was culturally different from the Hmong, and their religion was Buddhist. Once again they were welcomed in the community service programs run by the parish. (By this time sewing had been added to the curriculum.) As with the Hmong, religion was not pushed, although most of the Cambodians joined the parish. The instruction class now took on a different aura. In addition to the instruction being delivered in Hmong, it was now also given in Laos which many of the Cambodians understood, but which was not understood by the older Hmong women.

Indochinese people have now become active in many aspects of parish life. Hmong women have belonged to the altar guild for four years, as well as to the Daughters of Grace Church. The young people not only participate in church school classes, but also in the youth group, the servers' and lectors' guild, as participants in the diocesan youth conference, and church camp. A year and a half ago, one of the interpreters was elected a member of the Grace Church vestry.

In 1983, the Hmong Mutual Assistance Association was formed, and assumed the many tasks formerly performed by volunteers. Apartment finding, furniture hunting, landlord/tenant understanding was now administered by the H.M.A.

As an experimental project, members of the parish attempted a food service, in the form of a parish restaurant called "The Elegant Elephant." This weekly activity featured a bi-cultural menu and was heavily attended by Sheboyganites who enjoyed an ethnic flair, in addition to giving work credits to those who prepared and served the food. The Indochinese Society shared the profits. The service continues to this day as a catering service.

In 1983, some members of the parish and the community at large established a quality children's center in the parish hall. Under the patronage of St. Jude, the doors opened to embrace children of all races, with a bi-lingual and multi-cultural emphasis.

Last year, Benjamin Ber Lee, an interpreter from Grace Church, stood at the lectern of St. Paul's Cathedral, Fond du Lac, where he read a lesson in Hmong at the opening mass — thus marking the first such occurrence in the worldwide Anglican Communion.

Sheboygan plaza is still vacant and some of the industries have relocated in the sunbelt, but in a special way we are blessed with a refreshing new influence in our city. The Hmong have brought happiness and industry. They have responded to our concern as we have to them. Our parish has changed and we are "renewed in the Spirit."

For our friend Rudyard Kipling, perhaps East and West do not meet, here on earth. But for us — well, for us, we have experienced the miracle of the age — cultures blend as do the ages.

— Duane R. S. Mills

Ideas which this chapter sparks for possible application in our congregation:

Resources we already have in our congregation which could facilitate such a ministry thrust:

People in our congregation who should read this chapter — and who may be good candidates for a task force:

6 | Ministry With Senior Adults

Trinity Lutheran Church
Roselle, Illinois

"What'll I do if I retire?"

"I've done my share of work for the church. Let the young ones do it now."

"The church doesn't know I'm here. It only caters to the younger generation."

"Where'd all these old people come from?"

"I'm not ready to sit and rock! Give me something to do!"

"Nobody likes my ideas any more. The younger generation wants to do it differently."

"Here I am! What can I do to help?"

Sound familiar? Of course it does.

The response that Trinity Lutheran Church, Roselle, Illinois, makes to such common comments is its "Ministry with, by, and for senior adults." The special attention to active older members and others in the community includes a resolve never to underestimate the seniors — their interest and potential, their enthusiasm and creativity must never be discounted.

"Older" and "active," of course, are matters of relevance. If the event, program, or activity appeals, the word is "Come — and welcome!" regardless of age. No ID is required! Just recognize that it is planned with those in mind who are age 60 and up — those who are retired or semi-retired, those who are available especially for daytime activities, those who are comfortably active as opposed to the frail or housebound elderly. (The latter are served by other boards of the congregation, while the program here described is administered by the

Ministry with Senior Adults.)

How did it all begin? Trinity has made it a rule to look ahead and to anticipate needs — then have qualified personnel in place to develop a program, initiate and direct it as the need burgeons. Thus, a few years ago when the congregation saw its senior-adult segment of the membership growing faster than any other age bracket, the staff antenna went up to identify a qualified person to come on board as a part-time pastoral assistant (P.A.) specifically responsible for the senior-adult program.

The Lord directed to us a woman who planned to retire soon, at age 62, and who wanted to spend part of her newly-acquired free time in church-related work. While she was willing to volunteer, we felt it appropriate to provide compensation in line with that paid to other part-time employees of the congregation. (As it happens, much of what she receives is returned to the Lord's work in a variety of special gifts.)

Our P.A. began by preparing a description for a Ministry with Senior Adults, for approval by our church council. Goals set forth were to:

1. Assist the congregation in becoming more aware of the spiritual, physical, psychological, and practical needs of the elderly within the congregation and its neighborhood, and to work towards meeting those needs.

2. Assist the elderly in remaining an integral part of the congregation.

3. Assist the elderly in retaining their self-respect and active interest in life.

4. Provide opportunity for the elderly to use their talents and experience in the congregation and in the community.

5. Provide opportunity for the elderly to meet for mutual edification, education, and fellowship.

6. Assist the younger generation in preparing for retirement and later years.

7. Assist the younger generation in participating in those decisions that affect their parents.

Now, what are some of the ways we aim to meet these objectives?

Let's start with the Golden Agers Club. This is the one senior-adult program that Trinity already had in place, introduced by our congregation a few years earlier when the community began to recognize the need for some fellowship opportunities for the "golden agers" in the area. This is a community club housed at Trinity at no charge, and funded in part by the township and some local service clubs. Members also contribute $1 each time they attend. The Golden Agers Club meets on a given day each month, throughout the year, and functions with its own officers and treasury. The standard agenda is a short business meeting, dessert and coffee, and favorite card games (don't interfere with that play-time!). Twice a year they have a dinner, and only occasionally special entertainment; that's the way they want it.

Our P.A. fills an advisory and supportive role and serves as liaison with our own senior-adult events, and the pastor visits the meetings regularly, showing his interest and support. The Golden Agers Club has been left undisturbed by our Trinity program, other than that it has doubled in size (to over 100 members) since our own activities have been introduced.

What are some of those activities? The primary thrust of our senior-adult program is regular worship! We preach that, along with the Gospel. And Bible study is important, but many oldsters haven't grown up with that kind of experience and are hesitant to get into a group. That's why we key Bible study into what is now "Senior Monday," with the promise that no one is *required* to read aloud or to speak. But they do! The leader, usually the pastor, encourages participation by directing his remarks in a way that moves the seniors to make input about their experiences, feelings, attitudes, and younger days. It's also an opportunity for the pastor to develop a closer and more personal relationship with these folks, and they delight in having his attention in this non-class kind of setting.

For Bible study, we have provided several dozen large-print Bibles. In this way, all can use them without any individual feeling self-conscious — and we know they are appreciated.

How did "Senior Monday" and our other senior-adult activities get rolling? When our new P.A. came on board, she promptly began attending the Golden Agers Club meetings to develop a rapport with those folks, and very soon did a needs survey with that group. The results weren't especially surprising. Fellowship — being with other people — was the primary need, and that set the stage for future planning.

The P.A. first scheduled several quarterly fellowship gatherings. As a gimmick to attract the seniors to the first one, she planned a "goodies bag" — and made a big point of that, and the door prizes for the initial gathering. She contacted local merchants and services for inexpensive "freebies" and stuffed plastic bags with such things as rain bonnets, ballpoint pens, calendars, rulers, key rings, Social Security update brochures, reprints of health articles, refrigerator magnets, coupon offers, and the like.

Using a mailing list of our members age 60 and up, plus non-members on the Golden Agers list, a letter was sent by first-class mail to announce the gatherings and the features — the give-aways, refreshments, and entertainment, all free.

The response was excellent in numbers and enthusiasm. And it was an ideal time to distribute a check list of "What I'd Like to Have the Seniors at Trinity Do." This, then, became the basis for further planning.

Two more quarterly events were held, with refreshments and programs, and then it became clear that monthly recreational and sightseeing events were going to be the most desirable. So, for the gadabout type, we began offering Silver Streaks events. The calendar is planned by the P.A. for the folks who like sightseeing and recreational jaunts, plus a good restaurant meal.

Initially, when we had fifteen to eighteen participants, we car-pooled. When we began attracting twenty or more, we switched to chartering a school bus, which permits us to go farther afield. That is now our regular mode of transportation.

Where do we go? Our area, as a big-city suburb, is blessed with many and varied attractions. Here's a sampling: the zoo, big league baseball games, luncheon-theater, river cruise, historical society, museums, botanical gardens, specialty greenhouses, musical events. In four years, we have repeated only one event: the January annual "ice cream bash and games party," held in our own facility. It's a make-your-own-fantastic-ice-cream-creation and a table-game event.

The third Thursday of each month has become Silver Streaks day, and as nearly as events permit we schedule the trips for that day. They are priced at actual cost, lumping transportation, meal, admissions, tips. Each person pays the total fee when registering in advance. As nearly as possible, the Silver Streaks events are announced for a full year ahead, as far as date and event are concerned, with details publicized each month.

Recently we ventured into our first over-nighters, with a spring and an autumn three-day trip by chartered motor coach, and we look forward to some longer tours in the future.

With the Silver Streaks well established, we moved into the weekly Senior Monday program, briefly referred to earlier in connection with Bible study. Senior Monday continues, after Bible study, with a hot catered meal served cafeteria style for a freewill offering. The next hour is activity time — choose cards or another game, your favorite craft, visiting, or whatever. Sometimes a special program is planned by the P.A. — music, film, speaker. Finally, the last half-hour is devoted to exercise guided by a trained leader from our faculty. This could also be someone from a local hospital or "Y" or trained at one of those facilities. Non-embarrassing, non-strenuous, the exercise is geared to improving circulation and muscle tone and is constantly promoted as something to do regularly at home on their own. In spring we incorporate a group outdoor-walking segment.

Senior Monday has also been an occasion to develop some inter-generational relationship. We occasionally have the children of one grade of our school come in for the activity hour. They play games with the oldsters, provide a short program, or sometimes just visit in small groups.

Attending chapel service with the children is another inter-generational event. As the children, on their way to chapel, pass the gathered group of seniors, the youngsters take the hand of some older person and escort him or her into the sanctuary, so the seniors are scattered throughout the congregation and participate closely with the children in the service. These occasions have been highlights for the seniors, and the children also respond positively.

Senior Monday (or does another day fit your calendar better?) is a come-when-you-can/leave-when-you-must kind of event, but almost all attend for the entire three hours.

"How about funding?" you ask. As noted earlier, most activities are provided on a cost basis, and we aim to be considerate of those older folks who are on limited incomes. We have a few "angels" who anonymously cover the cost of occasional events for certain individuals. Without using names, we make such generosity known and in this way encourage others to assist financially. The annual congregational budget also provides a line item for senior-adult activities, and that might cover such things as an occasional speaker or musical program, a Senior Sunday memento, and the like.

Publicity for all of the senior-adult events is provided through special mailings, monthly congregational newsletter, weekly bulletin announcements, special flyers, local newspaper items, and announcements on local and Christian radio stations. One-to-one invitations are also extended by telephone calls made by members of the Ministry with Senior Adults.

To meet several of our other goals, this Ministry has also sponsored several pre-retirement planning workshops, and a seminar for family members who may have to provide care for older adults.

May non-members of our congregation enroll in any of these activities? Well, *of course* — why not? Nothing restricts us to socializing and serving, fellowshiping and sharing only with our own membership. So we open our programs to the community by inviting and encouraging the friends and neighbors of our members to share with us, to come and enjoy whatever appeals to them.

Is Trinity's program all fun and frolic? No! Many of our senior adults are involved in volunteer service of one kind or another. They serve on elected and appointed ministries and committees; do repair and maintenance work; help with Altar Guild efforts, including making paraments and baptismal napkins; do one-on-one tutoring and drilling in our day-school; serve as aides in classrooms and the library; operate the platemaker and printing press; in-put on the computer; mow lawn; serve as greeters; collate and address the monthly newsletter; usher; count offerings; do special mailings; keep miscellaneous records; videotape and edit; plow snow; telephone; plant and tend flower beds; teach Sunday church school; assist with meal service and refreshments for a variety of children's and adults' events; lector; sing in the choir; provide transportation; staff the Sunday morning nursery. What else? You name it — the seniors do it!

One Sunday each year the seniors are especially recognized and honored in the worship services, and at our annual volunteers' luncheon they constitute almost fifty percent of the attendees.

Have we gone about as far as we can go? Not at all. We still have a lot to be done! We know that as the years roll by, a larger and larger segment of our congregation will be in the 60-and-up bracket. We need to consider Senior Vacation Bible school, senior retreats, transportation needs, financial pressures, health services, and more and more ways for our people to serve — to feel important, useful, worthwhile. We want not to wear them out but to enhance their image, in the eyes of the others of the congregation, and especially in their own sight; to use their God-given talents and experiences in the Lord's service.

Among our objectives are two priority projects which we are studying — they're "biggies," but worth our effort: adult day care and senior-adult affordable housing. Long-term goals are to include suitable facilities for them in a future building program, if the Lord directs us into these projects.

To date, we know our program is practical and effective, because it attracts enthusiastic participation. And our sandwich-generation members say, "I can hardly wait to be a senior — all their special events and activities seem to be so much fun!"

— *Norma L. Thiemann*

Ideas which this chapter sparks for possible application in our congregation:

Resources we already have in our congregation which could facilitate such a ministry thrust:

**People in our congregation who should read this chapter —
and who may be good candidates for a task force:**

7 | Music Ministry

Saint Peter's Lutheran Church
Columbus, Indiana

A hum of excitement fills the music rooms and adjacent hallways. Quiet but hurried movement, low but urgent conversation fill the air with expectation. The mix and blur of color is reminiscent of the impressionism of a Monet, as robes of green, white, blue, red, and gold melt into each other in a continual flow of motion. The high, sweet sounds of a flute are heard from over in a corner, as the notes of a run are practiced; from behind a closed door come the quick, staccato notes of a trumpet; a minor chord, followed by its resolution into a major chord drifts from the handbell room. A little, red-robed girl rushes by in search of her mother; several green-robed men converse quietly, off to one side; a woman adjusts her neckpiece against her robe.

The director signals "five minutes"; the colors, like the movement of a kaleidoscope, swiftly sort themselves out, until all the same colors are together in lines. The director signals once more, and the procession begins, in hushed and orderly fashion, up the stairs toward the sanctuary. At the doors, the movement ceases. All is quiet. All is in readiness. Then, in one strong, resounding chord, the organ booms out its prelude to this glad celebration, and ordered lines of robed choir members begin their procession into the sanctuary, as the choirs and congregation together raise their voices. The trumpet adds its jubilation. The music blends, peaks, and becomes as one voice, in a glad, heart-felt proclamation of joy, filling the church, bursting from its outer walls, and floating into the cold, star-filled night. It has become as a host of angels singing from heaven.

Epiphany! The festival of the manifestation of Christ to the Gentiles! This is the one night of the entire church year when *all* of the choirs and instruments of Saint Peter's Lutheran Church blend together to celebrate God's gifts to humankind — God's gift of his Son, God's gift of his love, God's gift of his music.

The celebration of Epiphany is also the one night during the entire year when the choirs sing from the chancel and are seen by the congregation; at all other times, the musicians and vocalists are not seen; their music floats down from a rear balcony, as its intent is for worship, not for performance.

The Lutheran church has been a musical church since its founding; its heritage is rich in beautiful music composed by inspired writers. For Martin Luther, music was next in importance to theology; he thought of music as "the living voice of the Gospel." In emphasizing music as God's — not humanity's — creation and as God's gift to humanity to be used in Christian praise, prayer and proclamation, Luther laid the cornerstone for the inclusion of music of all kinds in the worship service of the Lutheran church.

In regard to the creation of music, Luther said:

> *Therefore accustom yourself to see in this creation your Creator and to praise Him through it.*
>
> *If any would not sing and talk of what Christ has wrought for us, he shows thereby that he does not really believe . . .*

Regarding the inclusion of musical instruments in worship, Luther encouraged all Christian musicians to

> *let their singing and playing to the praise of the Father of all grace sound forth with joy from their organs and whatever other beloved musical instruments there are.*

All music in the Lutheran church provides a path of

worship. Through music, God talks to us, and we talk to God. The purpose of the inclusion of the many different forms of music — the chant, hymn, chorale, motet, or anthem — in Lutheran services is that of worship, and its elevation to a higher inspirational level. In "Sing for Joy!," the Chorister's Handbook given to members of all choirs at Saint Peter's Lutheran Church, the following explanation is given:

> *We must understand clearly that choir work is a means of public worship. It is not a musical act, although it is musical. It is not a display of organizing skill, although it is organized. It is not a performance, although people witness it. It is* worship, *and this is a rare and special thing.*

Whether choral or instrumental, whether offered by the pastor, the choir, or the congregation, any musical rendition is centered on the liturgy. The music of a particular worship service must fit the theme for that day and season of the liturgical year; otherwise, it has no place in that particular worship service.

Saint Peter's Lutheran Church is fortunate in having many musicians and vocalists whose love of music adds to its three worship services each Sunday. All participation in the music ministry at St. Peter's is, of course, voluntary. Five choirs are included at different services throughout each month. The forty-member Adult Choir and the twenty-member Men's Chorus each sing twice a month, one Sunday at two of the three services, and the other Sunday at one of the three services. There are three children's choirs, each including from thirty-five to sixty members: the Sunday Singers, including students from grades three and four; the Laudate Choir, including students from grades five and six; and the Morningstar Singers, including students from grades seven and eight. Each of these choirs is included in one or two worship services each month.

The training of both adult and children's choirs emphasizes, first, the spiritual growth of the members, and secondly, their development musically. The Chorister's Handbook exhorts all choir members in this way:

> *The ideal choir singer is first of all a Christian in more than name. For him, Christianity is a way of life. He is a faithful servant, not primarily interested in himself, but is anxious about the welfare and happiness of others. He is able to realize that in all his service, he is serving "as unto God, and not to men."*

Our church is fortunate in having attached to it, both physically and spiritually, a day school, comprising Kindergarten through the eighth grade, which provides for the necessary time and logistics involved in the preparation of the three children's choirs. We are fortunate, too, in that the director of music for our church and his assistant are also teachers and choir directors in our school. Each of the three children's choirs rehearses for thirty minutes three times per week, during school hours.

We are also fortunate at Saint Peter's in having a music director and teacher who is, himself, a Christian example for both children and adults. It is obvious to even the most casual observer that he has a single-hearted purpose — that of serving God and his neighbor. His insistence on "singing the text" with understanding underscores the purpose of worship in each selection rendered by the choir. His love of children and gentleness in dealing with adults, even in the sometimes difficult situations encountered when dealing with choir members, affords a role model for children, an example of spiritual strength for adults, and makes a statement, by example, of the purpose of serving in a choir, of serving through the playing of an instrument, or of serving in any other way — to honor God.

Offerings by instrumental groups or individuals are also woven into the liturgy of the three Sunday services. The brass ensemble is composed of six men, each having other occupations and volunteering rehearsal time one evening per week; this group plays during services every other month. The adult handbell choir includes eleven women, rehearses one morning per week, and adds to the services every other month. The junior high handbell choir (involving nine eighth-graders) rehearses one half-hour per week during school hours and plays during services every other month. A harpist and several flutists play occasionally, either accompanying a choir or being accompanied by the organ.

The organ, of course, leads the congregational singing, as well as presenting attendant music, every Sunday during worship services. The goal of the organist, as of the various choirs, is not to perform, but to motivate worshipers to greater, deeper worship. At Saint Peter's, we have a moderate-sized, three-manual, Holtkamp pipe organ, which was donated as a memorial in 1962. With the expansion into a new church building, planning for which is presently underway, an up-grading of the organ is expected.

The introduction to and study of music in its many forms and the resulting understanding that it is a gift from God is possible at Saint Peter's through its day school. Students in the fifth grade may take beginning band and advance each year, up to the eighth grade. Handbell classes are offered during school hours to students in grades four through eight. A community organization offers a strings program after school hours. Each of these programs is offered at a time convenient to those students who may wish to participate in both an instrumental and a choral group. The music ministry of Saint Peter's includes both the church and the school; it is hoped that, through the variety of musical programs offered, students will come to an appreciation of music as one of God's most beautiful gifts.

The attempt in the planning of the musical portions of the worship services at Saint Peter's Lutheran Church is to achieve variety. Choirs sing at different services each time they are involved and may sing a cappella or be accompanied by the organ, by handbells, or by other instruments. The choirs add variety by singing special settings of various liturgical portions of the service, such as the "Gloria" or the "Sanctus." Handbell choirs, the organ, the brass ensemble, the flute, or the harp are woven into the fabric of the worship service, during the prelude, the introit, the gradual, the voluntary, the communion, during the singing of hymns, between the Bible readings, and for the postlude. Worshipers cannot assume that a certain service will always include a particular choir or instruments, as each Sunday is different.

The weaving of these various musical inclusions, of course, requires organization and planning, which, in turn, involves good communication between all involved. In this, too, we at Saint Peter's are fortunate. Planning for musical accompaniment during the worship services of the liturgical year takes place during the summer and involves our two pastors, the musical director and his assistant, the handbell director, and the brass ensemble director. More detailed revising and refining takes place on a weekly, or even daily, basis, as the year progresses. Following the initial planning of the summer, appropriate music is ordered and adequate time is scheduled for rehearsal, so that the finest praise of God possible by volunteer musicians may be achieved. In the selection of choir music, the goal is to obtain solid music of the highest quality, with meaningful texts, rather than texts which may lean toward the trite or sentimental. The performance of the musical portions of the worship services at Saint Peter's is not always perfect, since people are not perfect, but the purpose is never missed by those attending services or by those taking part in them.

One of the goals of the music ministry at Saint Peter's is, as in the church body itself, to include as many people as possible and to include all who may have the desire to join in praising God musically. Every singing choir or instrumental ensemble or solo is operated on a voluntary basis. There are no auditions; all who wish to offer their services are eagerly welcomed and appreciated for their commitment to serve. No organization can grow if it remains static; change is an essential element in growth. The music ministry at Saint Peter's is always open to new ideas and new ways to bring musical praise to God. Two ideas currently under consideration are the development and training of family choirs and the inclusion of a musical group of retired people. Each of these groups would have a special quality to bring to worship services, while at the same time, enhancing their own spiritual growth.

We, at Saint Peter's, fervently work toward a strengthening of the spiritual lives of those who participate in our music ministry and of those who benefit through the enjoyment of hearing God's Word proclaimed musically. We are, indeed, fortunate in having fine directors of music and willing church members who benefit themselves and others through their service. We fervently pray that the faith of the members of our musical family and the members of our congregation, who actively participate through their singing of the hymns and portions of the liturgy, will continue to be deepened through the study of the Word of God as clothed in music. We fervently hope for the enrichment of the inner life of each of those who study and enjoy worthy music.

But, above all, we are grateful that each one of us has the privilege of praising God and bringing other souls, as needy as our own, close to him, through music. Along with Martin Luther, we proclaim, "Music is the living voice of the Gospel."

— *Lynne Sullivan*

Ideas which this chapter sparks for possible application in our congregation:

Resources we already have in our congregation which could facilitate such a ministry thrust:

People in our congregation who should read this chapter — and who may be good candidates for a task force:

8 | Parish Education

First United Methodist Church
Oregon City, Oregon

First United Methodist Church in Oregon City has a commitment to growth through Christian education. We affirm Christian education's main purposes as spiritual nourishment, sharing the good news, and providing an experience of biblical community. All our energies go to developing classes that meet the needs of people — from Bible study to spiritual growth, from parenting children to current social needs, from infant care to groups for older adults.

In our faith community, we strengthened existing classes and formed new classes based on interest and need. We hope every student in every class will come to know Jesus Christ, will appreciate our biblical heritage, will experience rebirth and redemption, and will know the meaning of love and belonging through membership in a caring community.

Our growth started several years ago with a class for parents of children. This class, which is still offered, focuses on parenting from the Christian perspective. The group study suggests that parenting is most successful when principles of the Christian faith are brought to the challenges of guiding and caring for children. We have covered numerous topics and explored many issues. Here are just a few of the varied topics:

- Celebrating Halloween and All Saints' Day
- The meaning of St. Nicholas and Santa Claus
- Sibling rivalry
- Teaching children to pray
- Stress and burnout

• Creating family liturgies and rituals
• "Street-proofing" children
• Sexual abuse and children
• Kevin Leman's *The Challenge of Raising Kids,* video, 1983

The Parenting Class has brought many young families back into the church and introduced others to Sunday church school for the first time. In the past five years the class has grown from fifteen to sixty-five members.

Along with Sunday morning formal study, the class participates in outings to the zoo, potlucks, picnics, parties, and camping trips. Last Thanksgiving we experienced a retreat in the mountains, complete with turkey, two feet of snow, and the stomach flu. In spite of the flu, we have planned another retreat this year.

The class for parents of young children has utilized many books for in-depth study. Here is a partial list. Dorothy Corkille Briggs, *Your Child's Self-Esteem,* Dolphin Books, 1975, was a most helpful book. We spent several weeks reading and discussing James Dobson's *The Strong-Willed Child,* Tyndale House, 1978. Each year during Advent we focus for four weeks on how to celebrate Advent and Christmas in the home. Donald and Patricia Griggs have a most helpful book for teaching the meaning of Advent; their book is *Teaching and Celebrating Advent,* Abingdon Press, 1980. The The Parenting Class has helped us to join our Christian faith with the challenges of caring for our young. We are preparing a booklet of ideas from various members of the class to focus on family liturgies and events. If a family had a meaningful family birthday celebration, they will be able to share that celebration in the booklet with others. Another family can share some of their "secrets" about keeping children occupied in the car while traveling. The booklet is an opportunity to share "how to" events and ideas.

Each spring we hold a weekend retreat for all ages at the Oregon Coast. The retreat is especially for families. We gather for worship and study, for food and fellowship, and for recreation and fishing. There is plenty of time to "do your own thing," as well as for entering into serious Bible study. One of the highlights of the weekend together is a sand-castle-making contest where every sand castle receives a prize for originality and creativity.

Here is the story of one family. "My husband was at work, I was pregnant, and late," recalls Sally Smith, "but I wanted to go to a Christmas Eve service. I came to the Oregon City Church; it was packed.

"What impressed me most was a prayer to remember the policeman on the street. My husband, Wayne, was on patrol that night.

"I was just a Christmas-and-Easter church-goer at the time; Wayne had rejected his fundamentalist upbringing," she continues. "But when the twins were born, we wanted them baptized. We went back to First United Methodist.

"The pastor gave us a gentle reminder that baptism is a symbol of a serious vow: to bring up the children in the Christian faith. We started coming back to church — every once in a while.

"We heard the church was starting a parenting class, and we were hooked.

"Through the years we've added another child of our own, two stepchildren, and a foster daughter as well. Six children from age three to eighteen now live with us.

"We've been part of the Parents of Children and the Parents of Teens classes.

"Faith is such a moving force in my life now. My whole life is centered.

"I am a dispatch supervisor for the police department. The job is high stress and fast moving. I wouldn't even attempt to do it without my faith.

"From time to time I've been able to share my experiences from church, especially from my spiritual growth group, with the people I work with. They wouldn't always seem to be listening, but then they would see how my life has changed and they would inquire.

"Now, some of them are here in church and Sunday church school."

In an effort to stay current with members' needs and interests, we continually add new classes to our menu. For instance, we began a Parents of Teenagers Class because so many parents in the congregation wanted help in dealing with their adolescent children. Within this arena we offer support, information, spiritual strength, and the latest in books and film video. We have developed our own curriculum, utilizing such topics as the following:

- Kevin Leman video series on adolescents
- Love, sex, dating, and marriage
- Sibling rivalry
- What to do when your teenager won't go to church
- Peer pressure — media values
- Drugs and alcohol
- Teenagers and the Bible
- Parent-teen communication
- Parent-teen conflict
- Dating
- Discipline

Parenting a youth is a great challenge. The teenage years are packed with pressures, changes, problems, and excitement, and parents of teenagers need all the help they can get in guiding their children.

The purpose of this class is to help parents understand what it's like to be an adolescent, explore creative ways to communicate and handle conflict, share their faith and values with their children, and find support among other parents in similar situations.

As we developed our class agenda, we looked first at some of the more serious concerns facing youth and their families today.

Two resources that have also served as springboards for exploring the challenges of parenting are *Smart Girls Don't and Guys Don't Either* (by Kevin Leman, Regal Books, 1982) and *How to Live Almost Happily With a Teenager* (by Lois and Joel Davitz, Winston Press, 1982).

To understand the meaning of being parents, the class sought to identify the primary parenting tasks:

- Communicating effectively
- Sharing faith
- Explaining personal values
- Encouraging autonomy
- Nuturing self-acceptance and self-esteem
- Helping youth develop responsibility
- Guiding friendships
- Preparing teenagers for adulthood

A useful tool for carefully examining these tasks is *Adolescence Is Not an Illness* (by Bruce Narramore, Revell company, 1980).

As class members discussed their roles as parents, it became evident that one of their most troubling concerns was the constant level of conflict between parents and teens. Leaders try to help parents realize that creative conflict is possible even in families where hostile differences are common.

A good resource for studying conflict resolution is the article ''Defusing Parent-Teen Conflict'' by Catherine Morgan (*The Christian Home,* April 1979).

Another major challenge for parents is to understand what it's like to be a teenager. Our class has spent much time listening to youth and exploring what experts say about the teenage years.

Staying In Touch, a 6 part video series by Dr. Earl Wilson, 1984, has helped parents in our class shed their ''protective coating'' and take a close and realistic look at the world in which their teenagers live. Another good resource, *Teenagers Talk: Getting Through Adolescence* (available through EcuFilm) makes a powerful visual statement on the uncertainty and confusion of the teenage years.

Our Parents of Teenagers Class has developed what we like to call a biblical view of parenting. It consists of several principles, biblical in origin, that we believe Christian parents hold high:

- Parents are good examples for their children — emotionally, spiritually, and physically.
- Parents share their faith and beliefs with their children.
- Parents respect the views of children.
- Parents understand that children are a gift from God.
- Parents believe that family together-time is essential.
- Parents don't judge or harshly criticize their children.
- Parents listen with patience.
- Parents guide children with love, attention, and discipline.
- Parents present the model of Jesus Christ as a guide to their children.

Of course, not everyone is available for Sunday morning classes, so we also offer midweek study and support groups.

The Spiritual Growth Class is one such group. Members begin each session with a sharing time, continue with prayer and Bible study, and conclude with a look at the spiritual classics. During the course of the class, we have used such books as *Celebration of Discipline* (Richard Foster; Harper and Row, 1978), *Reaching Out* (Henri Nouwen; Doubleday, 1975), *Poustinia* (Catherine de Hueck Doherty; Ave Maria, 1975).

We have also increased our teacher recruitment and training efforts, seeking the most capable persons to lead our classes. We support our teachers by offering numerous training opportunities at the church and by encouraging attendance at district and conference events.

We dedicate the teaching staff during a worship service every fall. In June of each year, we set aside one Sunday for teacher recognition and thank-you's, including a special dinner for all teachers and their families.

There are other important factors that have contributed to our growth. For many years the Oregon City church has not had a summer church school (VCS). But we changed this three summers ago. We started a summer church school session and offered classes for all ages. The response was overwhelming. We have continued summer church school. For four weeks during the summer of 1982, we offered intergenerational interest classes. The response was enthusiastic. Besides classes for pre-schoolers, we offered the following classes: Adult Bible Class, Parenting Class, Folk Choir, Films from the New Media Bible Series, Interpretive Dance, and Mural Making. The last two months of the summer we offered more traditional classes in age groupings. Christian education all year round reminds everyone of the importance of a growing and disciplined faith, and it says to all that we take seriously such a ministry.

	Church School Membership	Church School Attendance
1972	238	130
1973	267	117
1974	245	130
1975	260	131
1976	259	133
1977	262	134
1978	255	134
1979	256	140
1980	314	155
1981	358	169
1982	417	193
1983	464	221
1984	498	245
1985	532	276
1986	555	328

Helpful and creative resources are important to any growing Christian education effort. We use the United Methodist curriculum fully and supplement it with resources from many different perspectives. We utilize films and filmstrips, records and cassettes, pictures and charts, posters and maps, and other media to help proclaim and clarify the Word we are teaching and sharing. The Genesis Project, *The New Media Bible* film series has been particularly helpful.

In the spring of 1981 we began to hear of the need in our congregation for serious and extensive Bible study. We started to respond to that need by assessing several approaches and curriculum for Bible study. We settled on the United Methodist *Genesis to Revelation* series. This series is an extensive six-year study. We recruited teachers and designed a registration form during the summer months. In August, 1981, we accepted registration for the Genesis study, and by the end of August we had seventy persons enrolled in five Bible study classes. Three of the classes meet on Sunday morning; one meets Sunday evening; another meets on Tuesday evening. All of the classes continue to be well attended and are solidly into the six year study. Each fall we add another Bible study class, so that new persons can begin systematic Bible study.

In the winter of 1982 we added another class. This class focuses on pain. Our Pain Support-Study Group meets once a month on Sunday evening. This class is for persons experiencing physical or emotional pain. We meet not only to share our experiences and to suppport each other, but also to study the dynamics of pain and how to cope with it.

The pain class has focused on such topics as: What is Pain?, Healing and Faith, Developing a Prayer Life, How to Meditate, How to Cope with Pain, and Divorce and Pain. The group has invited resource persons in to help the class focus on a particular issue. We have used the book by Philip Yancey, *Where Is God When It Hurts?,* Zondervan, 1977, as a study book for this class.

Brochures and mailings, newspaper ads, and stories clearly convey the excitement of our class offerings. Since the church has a message to proclaim — a great message — we try to share it creatively and aggressively.

Above all, we remember that Christian education is primarily spiritual education and enrichment. First United Methodist

Church continues to grow because we offer spiritual education and nurture for growing disciples — an opportunity we share with the entire congregation and the wider community.

Factors contributing to our growth:

- Pastors who are active in the church school (including ongoing teaching)
- Year-round church school
- Attendance goals and promotion
- Dedicated administrators and teachers
- Strong adult classes
- Midweek classes
- Personal visits, phone calls, and postcards to absent church school members
- Small classes
- Adequate budget
- Bible-centered curriculum
- Publicity and mailings
- Emphasis on a personal relationship with Jesus Christ.

In September 1985, we added two new adult classes. A class for Single Parents and a Spiritual Giants Class. These new classes have expanded our educational ministry significantly.

The Spiritual Giants Class offers highlights in the lives of Eric Liddell, Bishop Desmond Tutu, Mother Teresa, and Thomas Merton. Through the use of film, video, biography, interview, writings, and pictures we have brought these great persons of faith to life.

Through their lives, class members are challenged to greater faith. We looked at Eric Liddell through the Academy Award winning movie, *Chariots of Fire.* Liddell's book, *The Disciplines of the Christian Life,* has been central to our understanding of his preaching and teaching. A short biography in *The Adventurers* has been most helpful.

Tutu's two books *Hope and Suffering* and *Crying in the Wilderness* enabled us to understand the challenge and urgency of life in South Africa. Many articles in *Sojourners, The Christian Century,* and *The Other Side* have amplified his life and prophetic ministry.

Biographies of Mother Teresa and Merton serve our class study well. Their lives are also presented in extensive film and video offerings, *Mother Teresa of Calcutta,* LeJolly, 1983, is an excellent biographical resource to understand the life, commitment, and ministry of Teresa. A video portrait, *The Work of Love,* from Ave Maria Press brings her life dramatically alive.

In the fall of 1986, the Spiritual Giants Class focused on Martin Luther King, Jr., Dorothy Day, Ken Medema, Dietrich Bonhoeffer, and others.

Our Single Parents Class arose out of the need for several single parents in our congregation to get together for study and support. A large offering of resources are now available for such a class. *SOLO* Magazine is an excellent source for topics, discussion, and resource review. Video resources have enlivened this class. *Starting Over Single* video series from Prince of Peace Publishing, 1985, is one of the best resources for a Single Parents Class. Because we ran out of rooms, this class meets in a motor home which a member of the church parks beside the church each Sunday. Space is an increasing problem we face. But we can meet the space problem with creative planning. One of our Bible study classes has met in a doctor's reception room for the past two years. The office is only several blocks away from the church and serves well as a classroom.

Our educational vision looks to the establishment of an extension Sunday School in the Clackamas area. Clackamas is an unincorporated suburban city of 30,000 people, almost totally unchurched. Through a task force, we are planning to open an extension Sunday church school in a public school building or shopping area. We move forward because Christian Education is central to the church's growth and creates abundant living in the lives of all we reach and serve.

— *Wesley D. Taylor*

Ideas which this chapter sparks for possible application in our congregation:

Resources we already have in our congregation which could facilitate such a ministry thrust:

People in our congregation who should read this chapter — and who may be good candidates for a task force:

9 | Social Ministry (I)

Immanuel Lutheran Church
Palatine, Illinois

Keep the need in front of people, and they will respond.

That simple rule is the basis for a successful social ministry program. Immanuel Lutheran's congregation has found that basic needs for shelter, food and clothing can go unnoticed — and unmet — even in an affluent suburban community.

Members also have found that extending the church's social ministry effort to mission work in nearby areas where needs are even greater can produce dramatic results that are seen and felt by those contributing their time and talents to help others.

With a membership of more than 1,500 drawn from predominantly middle- and upper-income families, Immanuel Lutheran does not at first glance appear to be a church where any member would be without food, clothing, or money for utility bills and rent. But appearances can be deceiving.

Affluent communities often hide families and individuals thrown into sudden financial crises, with desperate needs not met by relatives, friends and neighbors, or the government "safety net."

Tim Hetzner, Immanuel Lutheran's director of Christian education, explains that the congregation's organized social ministry sprang up several years ago in response to such needs, and has grown steadily since.

Before Immanuel embarked on its formalized social ministry program, church members in a crisis often approached the church staff for help, usually as a last resort before utilities were cut off or a family lost its housing. Staff members responded by digging deep in their pockets, but the needs often exceeded the resources available.

In April 1983, Hetzner mentioned at a Youth Board meeting that a continuing need of the congregation was responding to members requesting help in such situations. The board established a "Good Samaritan Fund" with an initial balance of two-hundred dollars. The money came from four-hundred dollars already raised by young people of the church at their annual Easter breakfast.

"It seemed like a good way to put into action the biblical idea that loving God and loving others means serving God and serving others," Hetzner says. It was the beginning of Immanuel Lutheran's organized social ministry, which Hetzner defines simply as ministering to people who have hurts and needs.

Several important guidelines were established for the Good Samaritan Fund. First, all contacts were to be confidential. Second, cash payments were to be made only in crisis situations. Checks were to go directly to utility companies, landlords, or others demanding payment. Help was to be provided as a gift, not as a loan. "We discussed loans, but decided that was not what we wanted to accomplish through the Good Samaritan Fund," says Hetzner.

Finally, it was decided that no special fundraising efforts would be made for the Good Samaritan Fund. News of the fund spread by word-of-mouth. A brief item in the Sunday bulletin announced each week only the amount paid out of the fund to those in need — never the amount donated to the fund.

In its first nine months, from April to December 1983, the fund distributed slightly more than one-thousand dollars. In its second year (1984), the fund distributed a little more than three-thousand dollars. In its third year, the Good Samaritan Fund provided more than $17,000 in direct aid to both Immanuel members and others in the community, individuals facing personal or family financial crises.

Individual and family situations giving rise to need for help from the Good Samaritan Fund vary widely. The most common problem is financial strain in broken homes, Hetzner says. "For single mothers with small children, it's often a situation where the bills are backed up and the father misses a payment," he points out. In other instances, households which depend on a mother's or father's income as a salesperson are thrown into crisis when commissions don't come in time to meet monthly bills.

Because of rules regarding utility shutoffs for delinquent accounts in Illinois, the church has found that maintaining gas and electric service for needy families means dealing with a rash of shutoff notices whenever several days of warm weather follow a prolonged cold spell. During cold weather, utilities are prohibited from cutting off service, but they are quick to cancel service for past due customers once the weather allows shutoff notices after several warmer days.

Making payments directly to utilities or others demanding payment in a crisis eliminates most problems with potential abuses by recipients of gifts from the fund, Hetzner says. The church also collects food and clothing, which are provided to those in need and administered under the Good Samaritan Fund.

Hetzner is quick to point out that no one is ever refused food from the church pantry, but an informal network of local churches helps identify panhandlers and also helps prevent an unscrupulous individual from making the rounds from church to church in search of cash gifts.

Although there have been many occasions when the Good Samaritan Fund was drained, Hetzner says there hasn't been one time in more than three years of operation when a person in need was turned away because money was unavailable.

Most donations are put in the Sunday offering, marked for the Good Samaritan Fund. On more than one occasion, though, all the money received on Sunday was paid out by midweek. In each instance when that happened and another case arose requiring an immediate gift, money came in at the last minute to cover the need.

"The money always comes in — sometimes by a check in the mail, sometimes in an envelope slipped under the door," says Hetzner. "It has been a real blessing of the fund."

Hetzner says he and other church staff members occasionally share with a Bible study class or other church group how the fund operates and what the immediate needs are. "People get excited, because they know it's helping other people in our congregation or the community," he says.

Success of the Good Samaritan Fund has led to other, closely related social ministry activities.

When a family new to the community approached the church for help with furniture, a one-line item in the Sunday bulletin helped expand Immanuel's social ministry horizons from cash gifts in crisis situations to direct donations of non-cash items in non-crisis situations, as well.

The bulletin item responsible for the shift read simply: "Needy family has no furniture. In need of furniture." Response to the request was overwhelming. "All that week, we had trucks out picking up furniture," says Hetzner. So much furniture was donated that warehouse space had to be found. A church member with excess warehouse space for his business donated a warehouse for several months, until all the furniture was put in circulation again. "A lot of that furniture has been recycled two and three times," says Hetzner.

The church also coordinates minor home repairs and other small, service-oriented work for those with special needs that can be filled by congregation members. Home repair work is administered under the Good Samaritan Fund along with donations of food, clothing and furniture.

Large and small examples of the fund's helpfulness abound. A newly-married couple may borrow furniture from the fund's collection of used furniture. As they are able to buy furniture of their own, they return the borrowed pieces, which then are available to others with a need. Or, an older person living on a fixed income may need emergency plumbing or electrical repairs. These are handled through the fund as well, by coordinating the work of tradesmen who donate services and materials.

Operation of the fund has grown so that the church now is setting up a board structure to spread administrative work among members of the congregation with a special interest in it.

Hetzner sees the social ministry efforts at Immanuel Lutheran as a return to the longstanding tradition of Christian churches helping those in need. When the church fails to do the job, government steps in — with all its attendant problems, says Hetzner.

He believes that the mistaken idea of mission work as something done "anywhere but here" is a major cause of the shift away from social ministry and a decline in mission giving at many churches. "In isolated cases, churches now are returning to this responsibility," Hetzner says. As a remedy, Immanuel Lutheran has added close-in mission work to its social ministry efforts during the past year, supplementing distant mission giving, where results are seldom seen by contributors.

The first close-in mission project was undertaken early in 1986 in conjunction with sister Lutheran congregation Immanuel Houston on Chicago's economically depressed South Side, about 50 miles from Immanuel Lutheran of Palatine.

In recent years, Immanuel Houston suffered a decline in membership as the neighborhood changed from predominantly white to black and Hispanic. The racial composition of the congregation shifted with changes in the community, but the church's ability to support itself failed, leading to a major financial crisis late in 1985.

Immanuel Houston's need for help coincided with (Palatine) Immanuel Lutheran's desire to find a project in the Chicago area for close-in mission work. As staff members from the two churches discussed their problems and opportunities, a plan was formulated for helping Immanuel Houston through its immediate crisis.

In order to pay past-due bills, Immanuel Houston would

be forced to liquidate one of its few salable assets — the parsonage. However, that would leave the pastor and his family without a home, and the congregation without funds to provide other housing, even in a low-cost rental apartment.

As an outline of the situation emerged in discussions between staff members of the two churches, the decision was made that Immanuel Lutheran's contribution to helping solve Immanuel Houston's crisis would be to renovate a small, abandoned house on Immanuel Houston's property. A loan to pay Immanuel Houston's pressing bills was taken out, pledged against sale of the parsonage. Work on the new parsonage began almost immediately.

Immanuel Lutheran members raised $5,000 in cash and collected building materials donated by members and others in the community. Working with an architect from another church in the area, who donated his services, an architectural plan was drawn up for the renovation.

A week of intensive work by Immanuel Lutheran members commenced the Monday after Easter. An oak spiral staircase was donated at the last minute, improving the new parsonage's floor plan, but also requiring major alterations in the architect's plan. Unexpected structural problems necessitated additional effort and raised the cost by several thousand dollars.

Despite all the obstacles, a work crew of nearly 60 people (spread over one week's time) finished all the structural work and much of the finishing work in a concerted burst of energy that kept some workers on the job until after midnight several days.

At the end of the week's effort, a 72-year-old woman who had feared she would lose her church stopped to thank one of the work crew's leaders, saying simply, "You've saved our congregation."

To its already-successful social ministry efforts, Hetzner would like to see Immanuel Lutheran add family and youth counseling, and perhaps a visit to a third-world mission church someday. But for now, there's more than enough to do with programs already underway.

For those seeking advice on developing or expanding social ministry programs, Hetzner suggests starting with the words of Jesus from Matthew, Chapter 25. Describing who will be chosen on the side of the Lord on judgement day (verses 35-36), Jesus lists the simple human kindnesses that form the basis for all social ministry when he says, "For I was hungry and you gave me food, I was thirsty and you gave me drink, I was a stranger and you welcomed me, I was naked and you clothed me, I was sick and you visited me, I was in prison and you came to me."

Putting those words into action is a complete agenda for successful social ministry programs.

— Timothy R. Kellogg

10 | Social Ministry (II)

First Lutheran Church
Lincoln, Nebraska

When the Son of Man comes in his glory, and all the angels with him, then he will sit on his glorious throne. Before him will be gathered all the nations, and he will separate them one from another as a shepherd separates the sheep from the goats, and he will place the sheep at his right hand, but the goats at the left. Then the King will say to those at his right hand, 'Come, O blessed of my Father, inherit the kingdom prepared for you from the foundation of the world; for I was hungry and you gave me food, I was thirsty and you gave me drink, I was a stranger and you welcomed me, I was naked and you clothed me, I was sick and you visited me, I was in prison and you came to me.' Then the righteous will answer him, 'Lord, when did we see thee hungry and feed thee, or thirsty and give thee drink? And when did we see thee a stranger and welcome thee, or naked and clothe thee? And when did we see thee sick or in prison and visit thee?' And the King will answer them, 'Truly, I say to you, as you did it to one of the least of these my brethren, you did it to me.'

(Matthew 25:31-40, RSV)

This congregation shall live by faith active in love. It shall motivate, equip, and support its members to visit the sick, the infirm, and the imprisoned, and to minister to the poor and the distressed; to serve as Christians in all the institutions and structures of society of which they are a part; and individually and corporately to foster justice, overcome oppression, alleviate suffering, and care for the earth. In these efforts the congregation shall cooperate with the synod and the church-wide agencies of the Lutheran Church in America, other Christian churches, and other groups in society. It shall make certain that its other functions strengthen the motivation and ability for service.

(The Approved Constitution for Congregations of the Lutheran Church in America, Article III, Section 1, d.)

First Lutheran Church of Lincoln, Nebraska, is a traditional middle-class suburban church. It has created its social action program through keeping to a few concerns over a long period of time; picking issues which are not headline makers at the time when they are picked; and mixing education with gifts of money and time and direct efforts to influence the social community.

For example, in the late 1960s and early 1970s, Lincoln churches had developed a thorough concern for racial integration and justice as regards black Americans. However, the situation of Native Americans was more complicated at that time in that they had little in the way of a civil rights movement, lacked strong local leadership, and had a tradition of separatism which more demanded justice than integration. Indians were also at the bottom of every social welfare index: last in employment, wages, high school graduation; first in arrests. In the late 1960s local Indians decided to organize an Indian Center using OEO funds. Originally First Lutheran contributed expertise in writing the Center's by-laws and later funded its alcoholism program. When the Center had lost nearly all of its Johnson era "great society" programs, First Lutheran was nearly its sole support. Later when the Center got going again, the church provided seed money for new programs: for a halfway house program, a pantry, an education program, and recently a preschool. First Lutheran's former pastor, Harold Hamilton, took a leading role among Lutheran pastors in influencing the City Council to give the Center land on which to locate a new building. When the federal government nearly took away the Center's funding a couple years ago, First Lutheran sent a Center proposal-writing team to Washington, and it wrote a successful request for federal support. Church members served on the Center's mayoral financial task force. After a decade and a half, the Center is a stable institution headed by Sydney Beane, also the president of the National Indian Lutheran Board, an institution which serves over 1500 people annually. Further, out of the Center's work has emerged a native leadership group in education, business, and higher education which has allowed Lincoln Indians to adopt a leadership role in the whole area.

Food and agricultural justice have been a second long-term concern, and they were so before the currently-fashionable issues arose. In the early 1970s, First Lutheran's Social Action Committee sponsored the Lutheran Legislative caucus, a group of active citizens who sought to exert a Christian influence in legislative matters. The Legislative Caucus in turn secured the passage of a bill requiring the registration of corporate farms with the Nebraska Secretary of State. More recently, as the farm crisis has worsened, the citizens of the state passed a constitutional amendment forbidding corporate farms, but the legislature repealed the reporting bill which would have been a major enforcement tool. Now an intense effort is under way to restore the reporting bill and protect rural parishes through enforcing the constitution.

At the same time, First Lutheran began direct efforts in the food and hunger area — staffing pantries, participating in the CROP Walk, delivering Meals on Wheels to the elderly, collecting at first hundreds and later thousands of pounds of food for the local pantries, planting a church garden, and collecting surplus food from parishioner gardens. As this sort of quiet action grew, the social action committee organized educational programs about world hunger. For example, in the early 1980s Roland Luedtke led a study of Amos, and focused on the food and hunger issues which influenced him and all who took the course. When Mr. Luedtke later was elected mayor of Lincoln, he gave excellent support to the city's hunger programs in a time of declining city and revenue sharing budgets. The Amos study was followed by a biblically-based study of the causes of world hunger and its relation to American food and agricultural policy in Africa, South America, and elsewhere, based on Jack Nelson's *Hunger for Justice*. Ultimately the congregation sponsored a successful resolution at the Nebraska Synod meeting of the Lutheran Church in

America, asking congregations to give at least $3.00 per member annually to the World Hunger Appeal. First Church joined *Bread for the World* as a covenant church, the earliest in the area, and it has been followed by six other churches. It has a fifty-member quickline which encourages people to speak to national representatives and senators about food and hunger issues, and it has sponsored an annual offering of letters directed to those concerned with hunger legislation. Each year many sessions of the congregation's Christian education program are directed toward educating the congregation on food policy and hunger issues. This year's main adult sessions were a powerful series of lessons relating the bread and wine of the Eucharist to our sacred obligation to feed the whole body of Christ.

In seeking to chart its own course, First Lutheran has emphasized Namibia rather than South Africa, (leading in the development of a synod-wide Namibia study based on CIDOC research in the 1970s and subsequently supporting a Namibian lay minister). It has stressed Cambodian refugees more than Vietnamese. It focused on the Christian obligation in a nuclear age in the years before the current popularity of nuclear freeze resolutions in the churches. It is our belief that the church can work more effectively if it identifies issues of justice and social concern *before they reach the front page,* before they become partisan, before the congregation and community are polarized. The individual congregation's witness is also likely to be more powerful if it says the same thing faithfully, year in and year out.

First Lutheran's social action committee is not large, but it is hard working. Its membership has always included conservatives and liberals, and its support has always gone to Nebraska Synod, Lutheran Church in America, institutions and causes first. It has depended heavily on national social statements from the LCA for guidance and legitimacy. When it has taken on a unique issue, it has usually done so for an extended period of time with a combination of education, worship, individual parishioner gifts and personal action, and collective congregational speaking. If it has been successful at all, it has been so because it has understood that we are all one body in Christ and all the members do not serve the same function.

Twenty Helpful Suggestions

1. Have a social ministry committee (with a chairperson who is on the church council and a pastor in attendance at meetings).

2. Tap congregational resources.

3. Co-operate with local helping agencies.

4. Co-operate with the District/Synod of your denomination.

5. Seek resources from District/Synod and national Church.

6. Co-operate with other denominations.

7. Make benevolence giving the number-one priority in the congregational budget.

8. Access dimensions and profiles of your congregational ministry and diversify.

9. Encourage members to keep informed on social issues.

10. Challenge members to put faith into action through deeds of love and justice.

11. Challenge other congregations and Synod/District to take action on social issues.

12. Pick *a few* issue areas in which to specialize.

13. When possible, pick issues *before* they become big headline-makers and partisan stereotypes have been deeply established.

14. After choosing a specific social ill to address, look for people who are affected but are not getting headline attention. (Example: regarding racism in the 60s, we focused on Native Americans more than blacks and in the 70s/80s on Namibia more than South Africa; and Cambodian more than Vietnamese refugee resettlement.)

15. Hunger is a good issue with which to begin involving people in social ministry for several reasons.

A. Most people seem to be interested in it; thus it is not initially very controversial.

B. Hunger is interrelated with other peace and justice issues; thus it can lead to future involvement with these other related but more controversial issues (such as the arms race and economic justice).

16. *Bread for the World's* "Covenant Church Program" is an excellent way to begin involving people in more action-oriented structure-changing higher profile social ministry. (For information on this program write: *Bread for the World,* 802 Rhode Island Ave. N.E., Washington, D.C. 20018.) BFW also has excellent educational/worship-devotional resources.

17. Involve youth in social ministry, through church school, vacation church school, confirmation, and worship. An important way to reach adults is through their children, who are especially good at consciousness raising concerning important social issues.

18. Co-ordinate with your pastor(s), church council and

other standing committees, *especially Christian education.* It is almost better to have people committed to social ministry in the leadership roles in Christian education than on the social ministry committee. Many of our strongest supporters of social ministry have rotated off the social ministry committee precisely to bring social concerns to the wider congregation through education programming — adult and youth. In turn, people from education committees and programs have come to join the social ministry committee because of what they learned in educational programs.

19. First Lutheran has found a non-denominational monthly Christian magazine dedicated to social issues called *Sojourners* to be very helpful for two reasons. Not only does it provide us with excellent reporting on social issues and Christian resources but through their "subscribe a friend" option we have been able to help introduce people to social ministry. Subscribing for your pastor as a Christmas gift is an excellent way to introduce him or her to greater possibilities for social ministry. (For more information write to: *Sojourners,* Box 29272, Washington, D.C. 20017).

20. First Lutheran has found the booklet called *Social Ministry: A Congregational Manual,* offered by the Lutheran Church in America, to be an outstanding guide and resource for organizing and directing our overall social ministry program. (To order copies write: Parish Life Press, 2900 Queen Lane, Philadelphia, PA 19129.) We have found the exercise called "Analyzing Our Present Program" (page 28) to be extremely helpful as a means of assessment and evaluation. It involves people knowledgeable of the different ministries and programs of the church getting together and charting those of the congregation's total activities which have a social ministry impact. The chart is designed to show two aspects of any social ministry activity — "Dimensions" and "Profiles." An activity of a social ministry nature may take one of three

possible "Dimensions." It may be of a "Study" nature, a "Service" nature (which works through an already existing societal structure) or an "Action" nature (which seeks to change and improve the societal structure itself). Moreover, activities of these three dimensions vary with regard to their visible "Profile" (or degree of controversy). The following page contains a sample chart of some of First Lutheran's social ministry activities. A typical congregation might find itself with social ministry activities clustering in the upper left hand section of the chart (study and service projects of low and medium profile.) The goal of a congregation should be to develop ministries in all nine quadrants of the chart.

— *Steven C. Gilchrist*

Profiles	Dimensions: Study	Dimensions: Service	Dimensions: *Action*
Low	1. Bible study on *Amos* — hunger 2. Wrote stewardship program grades 1-6 & gave offerings to specific areas 3. VCS "Space for God" each day a social issue 4. Lots of Adult Forums on Social issues 5. Bishop Kiechter (Leipzig) spoke on Iron curtain	1. Meals on Wheels (27 volunteers) 2. Support Peace and Justice Week 3. Weekly Food Ingathering (52 weeks a year) 4. Support Indian Center with money and public testimony 5. Women in Community Service — support with money and hours of volunteer service	1. CROP Walk 2. Church School — Children made pictures and they were sent with three members to USSR (& 6 countries) and received response back 3. Sent Director of Indian Center to D.C. to ask for funding 4. Church testified to city about property for Indian Center
Medium	1. World Hunger Study Class *God's Food* (Communion and World Hunger) 2. Review and respond to first draft on LCA statement on Nuclear Arms race 3. Mr. Hatuchtali (Namibian) spoke 4. Fjedar Singers opposed to Apartied — also raised $200 for TV coverage & singing at Capitol Bldg. during Peace Week activities 5. Ed. Forum on demise of state funding of Indian & Women's commissions — articles monthly in newsletter.	1. Food Pantry — staffing and weekly contributions 2. LCW — over 100 quilts made to LWR; now making them for Bethphage (home for handicapped) 3. Support peace making workshops (Community events) 4. Resettlement and working with Vietnamese and Cambodian refugees (over 60 refugees resettled) 5. Benevolence giving to Synod and LCA 27% of budget	1. Bread for the World phone chain (50 people) 2. Support ½ time "missionary" in social work in Namibia 3. Bread for the World Covenant Congregation and related work
High	1. Peace issues & Bible study (several classes — have been controversial) 2. Lenten evening worship series Sanctuary movement Farm Crisis Central American South Africa Eastern Europe	1. 5% of budget goes to specific city & world-wide agencies (amount makes it controversial) 2. Send many resolutions (controversial) to Synod 3. LCA World Hunger resolutions (Synod) that each member contribute $3.00 up from 50¢ per member.	1. Offering of letters (BFW) (74 letters this year) 2. Supported and petitioned Synod resolution to city of Lincoln for Nuclear Freeze — have since taken this to Synod convention 3. "Freeze Walk" signed the pledges at church

Ideas which these two chapters spark for possible application in our congregation:

Resources we already have in our congregation which could facilitate such a ministry thrust:

People in our congregation who should read these two chapters — and who may be good candidates for a task force:

11 | Spiritual Renewal

Saint Paul's Episcopal Church
Darien, Connecticut

Darien, Connecticut is an affluent, sophisticated, quiet town of houses buried in trees and surrounded by well-clipped expanses of lawn. Primarily a "bedroom" community for New York City executives, there are no factories, no apartment houses or condominiums (although a condominium project for the elderly was recently approved, after a planning and zoning battle of many years' duration) and, to listen to the young people of the town, very little to do. Social life centers around dinner parties, or the six clubs for golf, tennis, swimming, boating and riding. One would think it an unlikely spot for the outpouring of the Holy Spirit and renewal in the Church!

Saint Paul's Episcopal Church in Darien was established only a little more than a quarter of a century ago, yet this comparatively recent birth has had its advantages in the work the Spirit has done here. A congregation arose that was seeking; a Rector arrived with new ideas; a lay leadership was raised up ready to accept and act upon the subtle direction of the Holy Spirit. Saint Paul's became, in effect, a church marked by change, growth and readiness to accept and adapt to the winds that blew upon it.

Originally a mission church, Saint Paul's became a self-supporting parish in 1965. When the Rev. Everett L. Fullam arrived at Saint Paul's on October 1, 1972, he found a more-than-usually-committed group of churchpeople in his flock, and a core group of Christians who had dedicated their lives to Jesus Christ, many of whom had experienced renewal in the Holy Spirit. On his first Sunday in Darien, Fr. Fullam stood before his new congregation and announced that he was not going to be the head of Saint Paul's; that God had made it clear to him that Jesus was to be the Head of the church, and that He would direct His Body. Terry Fullam knew, and stated to the congregation, that he was an instrument to be used to teach and lead the people in obedience to God's will, to accomplish God's purpose in that place.

Shortly after his arrival, Fr. Fullam announced that there would be no more every-member canvassing of the parish to solicit pledges for the church budget. The Lord's will would be accomplished in the budget, as well as in the rest of the ministries of the church. The congregation was told that their commitment of their resources was only an outward manifestation of their commitment to the Lord. If they had not made their commitment to Jesus as Lord and Savior, then they were instructed not to put a penny in the offering, because God cannot be bought. If, however, their substance was to represent an offering of the totality of their commitment to Jesus, then it was accepted as given, but not pledged in advance. The budget would be determined by the elected leadership of the parish, the Vestry, according to the needs they saw as important to do the work the Lord had asked them to do. The budget that first year, 1972, was a little over $26,000. The approved budget for 1986 fiscal year was $1,025,000, an increase of almost forty times over in fourteen years. Each year, the pledges are sent to the congregation for their prayerful consideration. On Covenant Sunday, the pledges are brought forward to the Altar and laid in a basket. At the end of each service the pledge slips are taken out into the parking lot, placed in a charcoal grill, and burned, as the congregation sings praises to the Lord. Then the finance Committee begins its recommendations to the Vestry, and the Vestry finalizes the budget for the year. The Lord honors His requests. Only twice in fourteen years has there been a slight shortfall at the end of the fiscal year, and each time the Vestry has gone to concentrated prayer to determine what priorities were missed, and corrective action has been taken.

As Fr. Fullam expounded and interpreted the Scripture in Sunday sermons, weekday teachings and Bible studies, the parish began to understand that the words of Scripture are as pertinent today as they were 2,000 years ago. Parishioners turned to the Bible more and more as they sought God's plan for them, and guidance in Christian living. For the many who had never read the Bible, their discovery of its content was a life-changing experience. As new people continue to join the fellowship, lives are continually being dedicated to Jesus Christ and his service. Members are urged to seek the dimension of renewal in the Holy Spirit as an enablement of power for ministry.

As the church learned to find its answers in Scripture, the concept of the ministry of the laity began to unfold and develop. Fr. Fullam never ceases to emphasize that the Body of Christ is meant to be a *community of ministers.* The ordained clergy were never intended to have *all* the qualifications necessary to minister to the Body. As Fr. Fullam has often remarked, if Saint Paul himself were the Rector, he could not accomplish all the things essential for the Body's health! Rather, the role of the clergy is to enable, train, and assist the laity in developing their individual ministries in service to the Lord and to each other. Ephesians 4:11-16 and Romans 12:4-8 spell it out clearly, and Saint Paul's people believe it. Every member is encouraged to seek the Lord's leading as to what his or her ministry will be, along the lines of the individual's own talents. There are *no* unnecessary talents in the Body of Christ, just as there are no unnecessary parts of the human body.

The parish motto is, "To Know Christ and to Make Him Known." Strongly scriptural in foundation, Saint Paul's sees itself as concerned with four basic biblical ministries — worship, teaching, caring and evangelizing. The ministers are the entire congregation, and God seems to bring people with special talents suited for the ministries he raises up, supplying answers to needs that are not being met. For instance:

- The tape ministry was brought from a hand-held portable

to a multiple production ministry when an NBC technician in the parish became deeply involved in preparation and production of the tapes of the service sermons. He also installed the closed-circuit TV for overflow crowds in the parish hall, and his wife and son continue his work today.

• When answering the telephone began to take up all of the time of the office staff, twenty-two women who have pleasant personalities, cool dispositions and a willingness to serve, signed up for a half-day each as telephone receptionists.

• A professional librarian organized the book library and another book lover gave the bookstore its start. Today the bookstore utilizes dozens of lay ministers who help the paid manager keep this thriving ministry operating.

• A woman who "only knows how to cook" started "The Family Table," which provides lunch every day to staff and visitors, assisted by dozens who can also "only cook" and be gracious hostesses. The Tuesday morning service is followed by a hearty, delicious lunch for 150 people so they can share in the fellowship of the Lord, and this lunch only costs them $2.00, a miracle in these inflationary times.

• Two doctors, psychiatrists, a dentist, several lawyers and accountants are always available to provide treatment and assistance to parishioners unable to afford professional help.

• Retired businessmen cope with individual cases of need, routing people to assist them.

• A committee of men, one of whom is a builder, oversees the repairs necessary to keep the church plant running smoothly.

• Musicians offer their talent to enhance worship. The list goes on and on.

One of Saint Paul's goals is to be a "caring community," as the Lord leads, and to whomever he brings. The caring ministries take many forms, informal and formal. A many-linked prayer chain is lovingly shepherded by a lay person. The pastoral coordinator is a woman of the parish who meets with the clergy three times a week to facilitate the hospital, shut-in, and elderly visitations, and consults on the more practical concerns in the parish. "Needs and Deeds" puts people in touch with sources, both in the congregation and in the community. Another activity is the "Helper" program. Each Tuesday evening members go out and minister to the first-timers to Saint Paul's, and to others who request a visit.

As the needs of the Body of Christ have been met, Saint Paul's has moved into a wide area of outreach beyond its doors. Fr. Fullam has said that "the church exists primarily for those outside of it," and so groups of people who have a talent for loving the old, the crippled, the mentally ill and the imprisoned, make weekly trips to convalescent homes, a private and a state mental institution, men's and women's prisons and a "youth facility" for incarceration. They lead worship services, Bible studies, spreading the love of Jesus around in otherwise dismal surroundings. Individuals give innumerable hours of service to local charities, such as shelters for the homeless, feeding programs for the poor, and camps for inner city children. Countless neighborhood Bible studies are held in homes. Saint Paul's supports 24 missionaries, in 20 different organizations, and has a program for support of parishioners who seek to become ordained as Episcopal priests.

Perhaps Saint Paul's most significant ministry has grown from following the motto of the church, "To Know Christ and to Make Him Known." Although the members of the Body do not all have a ministry of evangelism, Scripture is clear that all should bear witness to their faith. Learning to express their own experience of Jesus' saving grace is not easy for "God's frozen people," but the clergy continue to provide opportunities to parishioners to practice this expression. Members are urged to take part in Faith Alive Weekends, and in Tres Dias, an ecumenical expression of Cursillo (a spiritual enrichment ministry). Classes are held for New Christians, and part of the course entails developing a three-minute testimony, to have ready at any time, in fulfillment of 1 Peter 3:15.

As a means of assisting renewal in other parishes, since 1976 the church has held "Parish Renewal Conferences" attended by parish groups from all over the country and Canada, crossing all denominational lines. Up to 200 visitors are accommodated at these weekends, staying in parish homes and attending teaching sessions, workshops and services. Attendees share in the discussion of problems and challenges of revitalizing divided, faltering, or dormant congregations. The whole parish mobilizes for these events, and everyone's talents are needed for the weekend's success. This early format has been revised to comprise three times a year, "Clergy Renewal Seminars" attended by ordained and their spouses, followed by three "Lay Leadership Weekends", when the clergy return with the lay leaders of the church.

A natural outgrowth of these meetings has been "Parish Renewal Outreach." Fr. Fullam's teaching gifts were recognized by the Vestry to be a gift to the wider church, as well, and he now spends as much as 65% of his time teaching at conferences and in churches all around the world, sowing seeds of scriptural foundation for renewal. He often takes laymen with him, to speak from their special point of view and to help with prayer and counseling. Scotty Clarke is Lay Minister for Renewal. He is responsible for the overseeing of the conferences at Saint Paul's and for the teams of laypersons which go out from Saint Paul's to parishes with special needs. Scotty and his wife, Phyllis, travel most of the year, as does another layman, Lee Buck. A parishioner first, Lee Buck is known around the world as an evangelist, enabler and teacher. There are many others. As the need arises, the Lord sends forth the people he has prepared here.

The most recent part of that preparation is the formation of "Jerusalem Conferences." These conferences were born out of the realization that, as the ministry of the church grew, a constant turnover of members was occurring, largely due to corporate transfers. The leadership was concerned that a common ground for old and new members be established, common teachings to prepare all for a common life in the Spirit.

Several times a year, a group of up to 72 parishioners will be gathered to grow in the Lord and in knowledge of one another. These conferences are led by the Rev. C. Gilford Green, who is given the title "Vicar" to point to the fact that he is charged with the supervision of the day-to-day operation of the parish, thereby freeing Fr. Fullam to travel as extensively as he does.

No two churches are alike, and what works for one does not necessarily work for another. Each is called to ministries unique to its situation and demographic makeup. Saint Paul's has had a large influx of young married couples and singles, and the need for a focus on discipleship and family ministry became evident. At the leading of the Lord, the Vestry authorized the hiring of two staff clergy for these foci. A young priest, the Rev. S. Mark Browne, agreed to move his family from Texas in answer to the Lord's call to become Saint Paul's first minister devoted to Youth and Young Adults. The Rev. Peter Church, originally a South African, was selected to become the first Minister of Discipleship. Although he is not an Episcopal priest, all agreed that he had the best qualifications for the need and was called to this parish. He is ordained a Methodist minister, but Saint Paul's realizes that God has no favorites. His blessings of joy and love are available to all who seek Him. This is the message of Scripture, and members of Saint Paul's seek to make it their own message.

Saint Paul's has no magic formula to offer to other churches. Its people testify only to their own corporate and personal experience of renewal and growth as a result of the submission to the headship of Jesus Christ and obedience to the leading of the Holy Spirit. There have been some false starts, some enthusiasms that did not last over the long run, but no "mistakes." Saint Paul's people believe that whatever is done under God's leading or while seeking his will is productive. Lessons are learned from seeming failures, character is built, individually and corporately, and God redeems errors as the church submits to his headship.

Renewal in the Holy Spirit is available to all churches, all individuals. Saint Paul's, Darien, Connecticut, seeks to be an instrument to help others step out in faith to be what God wants them to be — people commited to his will and purpose. Through his Holy Spirit, this parish seeks only "To Know Christ, and to Make Him Known." The ways in which that purpose is worked out is up to Him.

Lynda Barnes

Ideas which this chapter sparks for possible application in our congregation:

Resources we already have in our congregation which could facilitate such a ministry thrust:

People in our congregation who should read this chapter — and who may be good candidates for a task force:

12 | Youth Ministry

Covenant Presbyterian Church
West Lafayette, Indiana

God uses young people in mighty ways. Josiah was eight years old when he became king and by age fifteen he began to seek the God of his father David. At twenty he began to purge Judah and Jerusalem of idols and cast images. (2 Chronicles 34:1-4) Young people are strong and yearn to accomplish things of lasting value. The boy Samuel ministered before the Lord under Eli. The Lord was with Samuel as he grew up and all Israel recognized that Samuel was attested as a prophet of the Lord. (1 Samuel 3:1, 19-20)

Ninety-eight percent of the graduating seniors from our local high school pursue higher education. Each year several graduating seniors from our youth group pursue a full-time ministry vocation. In ten years these young people will literally be around the globe. Thousands of people will be touched by the gospel through these workers for Christ who have been sent from our youth group.

Effective youth ministry challenges youth to become workers for Christ. "The harvest is plentiful but the workers are few. Ask of the Lord of the harvest, therefore, to send out workers into his harvest field. Go!" (Luke 10:2-10) Often this command is applied only to adults. But God uses young people in mighty ways.

When I began in youth work I committed myself to God's sovereignty acknowledging that "no one comes to Christ unless the Father draws him." (John 6:44) It is by God's grace that any inherit salvation and grow to be workers for Christ. Yet our Lord's plan was to train a small group of men who could make disciples. My plan should utilize the same discipling principles as Christ's to build youth as workers for him. So my first task as a full-time youth worker was an in-depth study of the gospels. I studied to learn what types of things Christ did to train his men. The principles Christ used were precise and consistent. The things Christ did to train his men can be categorized into four areas: acts of love, contact, teaching, and sending. These four areas of activity have become the organizational model for the youth ministry at Covenant Presbyterian Church. The overall goal is spiritual growth in youth.

Acts Organizational Model

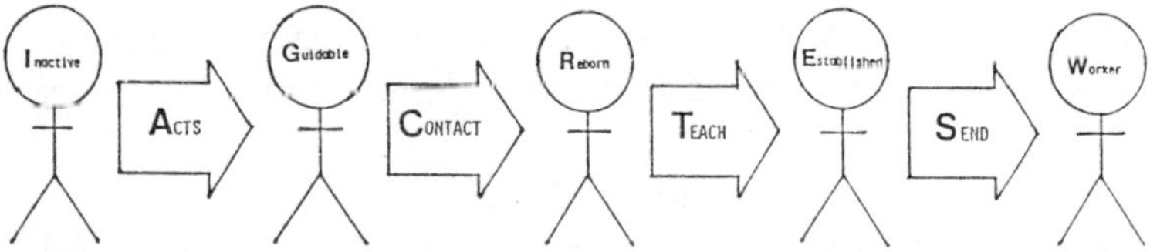

Acts of Love

We smashed it, stretched it, bent it, twisted it, sucked it, and still that gummy bear would not fall down. We discovered the elasticity of gummy bears that day at Arbys — and much, much more. It was the first personal contact I had with Eric. Eric was a fun-loving tenth grader. My agenda for our first meeting was simple; show Eric I loved him enough to take an hour out of my hectic day to talk and have fun with him. Eric is now a freshman in college. From that first day at Arbys until now Eric has started Bible studies, led many people to faith in Christ, and has gained respect in our church and community as a Christian who thrives on helping others. Eric's goal is to be in full-time work for Christ. He is a young man who has responded wholeheartedly to the call of Christ to become a worker.

My action of taking Eric to lunch and defacing gummy bears showed Eric I loved him. I sent Eric a card to thank him for the good time at Arbys and to say I enjoyed getting to know him. Several weeks later Eric developed serious girlfriend distress (SGD is a common symptom among teenage boys). He called me to talk because he knew I cared and loved him. Through such times Eric began to trust me. By now he knew my life was centered on Christ, so he was receptive to being guided by God's word and my counsel.

My acts of love to Eric did not happen by chance. They were deliberate efforts to share the love of Christ. Love in action is where Christ began with his disciples. Before Jesus called Peter, James, and John he filled their boats with fish. (Luke 5:1-11) Fishing was their life. It was their sustenance. Yet on that day Peter, James, and John had a need. They were discouraged and frustrated. Our Lord met their need through an act of love. They were astonished. They were ready to be guided by Christ for they pulled their boats up on shore, left everything, and followed him. (v. 11)

Christ's first interaction with people was often an act of love. The paralytic in Luke 5, the deaf and dumb man in Mark 7, the invalid by the pool in John 5, and the adulterous woman in John 8 all met Jesus through an act of love. Jesus acted out God's love first and then challenged people to follow him.

This principle is the first activity phase of our youth ministry. The goal of an acts activity is to guide spiritually inactive youth to Christ by sharing acts of love. Through our acts these spiritually inactive youth will become spiritually guidable.

Acts Activity Phase

We have a group of six to ten youth called the Acts Team. The goal of the Acts Team is to guide youth to Christ by sharing acts of love. Each member of the Acts Team has a specific ministry assignment to love others. One girl's assignment is to be a Barnabas. She sends cards of encouragement to her peers. Another is a greeter who informally greets youth as they enter the meetings. Our squatter sits by youth at group meetings that he doesn't know well or who are usually loners. One girl is a clique-buster. She roams around and pulls kids out of cliques to help them interact and make new friends. Other assignments include a phoner, taxi driver, complimenter, and birthday girl. Each fall at the Acts Team callout, members brainstorm new assignments to demonstrate Christ's love in action. The Acts Team's theme verse is 1 John 3:18, "Dear children, let us not love with words or tongue but with actions and in truth." Through these acts of love new youth experience Christ's love before they're told about it. Once a person has experienced Christ's love, they are ready to be guided to Christ.

The Acts Team also plans special events for the entire youth group such as ski trips, retreats, canoe trips, and movie nights. The goal of these special events is to guide youth to Christ through acts of love.

Acts of love is pre-evangelism. It is where discipleship begins. I have seen many teenagers turned off because they were told about Christ's love before anyone shared Christ's love with them. To teenagers this is hypocrisy and one of a teen's greatest longings is to know people who live what they preach.

I've learned this lesson many times. One was with Tom, an eighth grade boy whom I met at a fall retreat. Tom approached me after a gospel presentation and said, "I know I'm lukewarm. I want to grow and be hot. Will you help me?". It was my fourth month as a full-time youth director and Tom's words made me salivate. He was a hungry youth and I couldn't wait to dump truck loads of theological truth on him. I suggested we meet once a week for Bible study and prayer. During our weekly time I taught Tom all the insights God had given me from 1 John. Tom lost interest after three weeks. I was hurt and depressed. What had I done wrong? I forgot to love. I was so excited at the chance to teach Tom the meat of the Scripture that I forgot to love him. The time we spent was more benefit to my ego than to help Tom grow. I didn't even know Tom's interests or anything of his background. Tom stuck with youth group in spite of me and about a year later we talked again. This time my agenda was to love him. Tom's hunger to grow returned, and today by God's grace, he is a leader in our youth group.

Christ never ceased to love in action. All through his ministry, and at every phase of training, Christ served the disciples through acts of love. In Luke 8:22-25, when the disciples were gripped by the fear of the storm, Jesus responded to his disciples and close friends with an act of love. Christ culminated his ministry with the ultimate act of love by dying on the cross. Acts of love must never cease but continue throughout the ministry process.

Contact

Jesus asked a group of guidable men to come to him that they might be with him. (Mark 3:13-15) He needed contact with them to train them to be fishers of men. (Mark 1:17) The disciples were reborn through faith because the glory of God was revealed to them through their contact with Jesus. (John 2:11, Matthew 17:1-13)

As ministers of the new covenant we are called to reflect the Lord's glory with unveiled faces. (2 Corinthians 3:18) Through contact with Christians, others will come to know Christ as his glory is reflected. Several years ago, I was asked to identify the five most influential sermons I'd ever heard. I could only think of three. When asked to identify the five most influential Christians, I quickly thought of five significant persons who were models of the Christian faith. Teenagers will accept the Christian faith as they see it positively acted out in the lives of mature Christians.

Last summer I traveled with fifteen youth to Wyoming for a high adventure camp experience. Jackson, Wyoming, is a thirty-hour drive from Lafayette, Indiana. This extended time in a van produced some interesting conflict. The actions of one boy irritated several youth and adult workers. During the week these unacceptable actions continued despite warnings from the adult staff. The youth were watching to see how the adult leaders would respond. The conflict between the youth and an adult worker named Jerry came to a climax one night through a verbal shoot-out. The next morning several adult workers prayed about the problem. Jerry then apologized for the way he talked to the boy — without condoning his inappropriate actions. The rest of the week Jerry concentrated on unconditionally loving the boy and seeking reconciliation. The week ended with the two having grown into a positive relationship.

What interested me was how others in the group watched to see how Jerry would respond. It was a difficult situation, and they needed direction on how to act. Their contact with Jerry showed them Christian love in action. They could see a reflection of Jesus. They saw that God's way works when we yield and follow Christ. This contact experience built their faith in Christ more than most lessons out of a Sunday school book.

Contact is a key principle of discipling and is the second activity phase of our youth ministry. The goal of a contact activity is to help guidable youth be reborn in Christ through contact with Christian fellowship and biblical teaching.

Contact Activity Phase

Our Senior High group gathers every Sunday night for a meeting called Contact Point. Each year the teenagers identify eight student leaders based on biblical qualities of leadership. These eight youth plus several adult workers form the leadership team for Contact Point. The team plans all the activities, music, and teaching topics. There is time before and after the meetings for the leadership team to share and mingle with others. Leaders try to get into spiritual conversations and share their faith with others. Also, during this time the Acts Team youth are roaming around acting in love. Our goal is that youth will meet Christ through contact with Christians, biblical teaching, and a Christian love atmosphere. Through prayer and further contact our expectation is that they will be reborn through faith.

A key to contact work is the maturity of adult and student leaders. Most of my time as Youth Director is spent building the lay leadership in their faith and spiritual maturity. I meet every week with the Contact Point Team for Bible study, prayer, and evangelism training. As the team grows in their contact with each other, Christ, and the Scriptures, they are equipped to bring others to faith through contact evangelism.

Teach

Jesus Christ was the master teacher. He taught his disciples to pray (Luke 11:1-13), to be servants (Matthew 20:20-28, John 13:1-17), to persevere under persecution (John 15:18-21), commitment (Luke 14:25-34), humility (Luke 18:9-14), obedience (John 14:15-31), how to receive God's word (Mark 4:1-20), and much more. Christ was the perfect model of everything he taught. "I have set to you an example that you should do as I have done for you." (John 13:15)

Experts in learning have recently discovered that people learn best by another's example (this brilliant revelation has been known for thousands of years). Youth workers must set an example of receiving the Scripture, prayer, service, and obedience that is consistent with their teaching. "Can a blind man lead a blind man? Will they both not fall into a pit? A student is not above his teacher, but everyone that is fully trained will be like his teacher." (Luke 6:39-40) The point of this little parable is: get *your* act together before helping other people get their act together. It is a frightening truth. The youth I disciple will be like me.

My wife and I served as youth workers at a church in Ohio for two years. The youth in that church were longing for significant, adult role models. My wife and I each carried a 5½" x 8½" black, three ring quiet time notebook containing journals, study notes, and prayer requests. As we began to teach, we soon noticed several other black, three ring notebooks. Within a year the group asked the church to buy three ring notebooks for each member. They specifically requested 5½" by 8½" black, three ring notebooks. Some even learned what to put in them. The point is, they developed their personal quiet time after the pattern of their teachers including the size, type, and color of their notebooks.

Often youth workers inappropriately thrive off of this teacher/pupil relationship. The feeling of worth and security that this relationship brings is dangerous. The balance point is difficult to determine. Youth will learn by our example, but the goal of teaching must be Christlikeness, not a relationship.

In Phillipians 4:8-9 Paul says, "Finally, brothers, whatever is true, whatever is noble, whatever is right, whatever is pure, whatever is lovely, whatever is admirable — if anything is excellent or praiseworthy, think about such things. Whatever you have learned, or received from me, or seen in me, put into practice." In verse nine the things Paul refers to that they learned, received, or saw in him are the Christlike qualities in verse eight. Paul is not saying whatever sin or bad habits you see in me — put into practice. Paul wanted the Philipians to be like Christ. A student will be like his teacher. If the goal for the student is Christlikeness, then the teacher must exhibit Christlikeness.

The apostles became established in Christ's likeness because of God working through the Holy Spirit and the teaching of their master, Jesus Christ. To be established in Christ is to be set firm or rooted in him (Colossians 2:6-7, 2 Peter 1:12). Timothy was sent to strengthen and encourage the Thessalonians in their faith so that no one would be unsettled (1 Thessalonians 3:2-3). Jesus said, "If you continue to hold to my teaching, you are really my disciples." (John 8:31) The message of Scripture is the gospel of Jesus Christ and by this gospel young believers will be established. (Romans 16:25-27)

The goal of a teach activity is to establish reborn youth in their faith through teaching biblical fundamentals.

Teach Activity Phase

I meet weekly with a group of adult teachers committed to spiritual growth and Christlikeness. These teachers write personal, spiritual goals in the areas of Bible reading, study, memorization, prayer, and service. I hold the teachers accountable and encourage them to achieve their goals. In turn each teacher leads a small group of teenagers every Wednesday night. The small group members write personal goals in the four areas. The teachers encourage the youth and help them achieve their goals. The youth learn to build their lives on the Scripture. In time they become rooted and established in Jesus Christ. These established Christians are ready to be challenged as workers for Christ.

Send

Jesus sent his disciples as workers several times during their training. (Luke 10:1-17, Matthew 9:37—10:20, John 20:21, Matthew 28:19-20) In Matthew 10, they were given specific assignments to preach and perform acts of love. (Matthew 10:7-8) When the twelve returned, Jesus went away with them for an evaluation time. (Luke 9:10)

We can teach youth to share their faith and love others, but until they are sent out to do it, they haven't really learned. A teenager can only learn so much about driving a car in the Driver's Ed classroom. He hasn't learned to drive until he's been behind the wheel. Established Christians should be sent to minister as workers. The goal of our send activity phase is to develop established youth as workers by sending them to minister.

Send Activity Phase

On Wednesday night each of our small groups develops, organizes, and carries out one ministry project per semester.

These projects include prison ministry, convalescent care, evangelistic outreach projects, music ministry, ministry to latchkey children, and others. The youth are sent in much the same way Jesus sent the twelve and the seventy-two. Youth develop as workers when they put their faith into action outside the comfort and security of the church building.

Established Christian youth open to God's call for workers are also given the opportunity to minister through the Acts Team and the Contact Point Team. Through involvement in these ministry teams, youth are sharing Christ with their peers. When a youth grows in his faith to the point where he can help others grow, discipleship is occurring. This is the goal of our youth ministry.

The true test of teenage workers is after graduation, when they are sent from our youth group to unfamiliar and sometimes harsh circumstances. Will they be able to stand firm established in Christ? Will they be able to proclaim Christ to those with whom they have contact through their lifestyle and verbal testimony? Will they be able to share God's love in action and be used by God in mighty ways? I return to the illustration of Eric, the gummy bear persecutor.

After Eric graduated from youth group, he spent the summer working on a railroad spray train. Spray train crews are made up of tough individuals. Crew members travel hundreds of miles each week, work long hours, stay in sleezy motels, and do not enjoy the security of home for months. Eric had lived a relatively sheltered life so I was concerned about the vulgarity, immorality, and substance abuse he would face. Eric was also concerned, so we prayed hard before he left. When he returned one of my first questions was, "How did you handle the pressure and still hold up a witness for Christ?". Eric said that his crew members hit the bars and planned immoral activity on the second day he was with them. Eric knew he had to take his stand for Christ right then. He said to the others, "Wait a minute guys, I don't do that stuff." When the crew members asked why, Eric said, "Well, I'm a

Christian, and I choose not to do those things.'' Eric stood firm and didn't compromise his convictions. He was able to love his crew members even though he didn't accept their behavior. The crew members respected Eric and his faith. His verbal testimony and acts of love made an impact even though he was only with them a short time. God used Eric in a mighty way.

The key to the A-C-T-S organizational model is continuous acts of love. Christ never ceases sharing acts of love, and he calls his workers to act in love throughout their entire ministry.

Acts Organizational Model

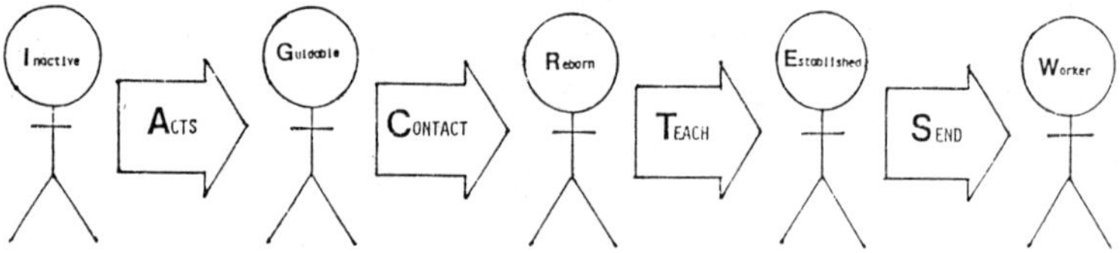

If we minister through A-C-T-S (*A*cts, *C*ontact, *T*each, *S*end) of love those we send will say ''I GREW'' (*I*nactive, *G*uidable, *R*eborn, *E*stablished, *W*orker).

— *Matt Boyers*

Ideas which this chapter sparks for possible application in our congregation:

Resources we already have in our congregation which could facilitate such a ministry thrust:

People in our congregation who should read this chapter — and who may be good candidates for a task force:

Reader Response

After you have read the essays in this book, you may find yourself saying, "Wait a minute! They should have included Saint-James-by-the-Supermarket. They're a great example of ministry excellence."

If you know about one or more congregations which in your opinion deserve the description "flagship" (including, perhaps, your own) please share this information with us. You may use the form below. Or, not wishing to deface the book, you may wish to create your own form (or simply put the information into a letter). Or feel free to photocopy this page.

I suggest you contact this congregation for a possible inclusion in a future volume of essays on Ministry Excellence:

Congregation ______________________________

Mailing Address ____________________________

City, State, Zip______________________________

Pastor's name ______________________________

This congregation demonstrates Ministry Excellence in the specific area of ____________________

Individual (if other than the pastor) responsible for leadership in the area of specific ministry named above ____________________

Form submitted by (Name, address)____________________

____

(For additional nominations, use the reverse of this page, or a separate page)

Send this form, please, to:

Editor, EXCELLENCE IN MINISTRY
C.S.S. Publishing Company
628 S. Main Street
Lima, Ohio 45804